D0475421

Top with Cinnamon

BY IZY HOSSACK

[CONTENTS]

I suppose that growing up in my household, with two food-loving parents, it was inevitable that cooking would become a major part of my life. Throughout my childhood I spent a large proportion of time in the kitchen at the countertop: starting out in a baby chair that clipped onto the counter, progressing to actually sitting on the counter, then standing on a little plastic stool so I could reach the counter. I'd help my mum bake, having the ever-important jobs of:
a) adding vanilla extract to batters (there was an incident with brownie batter once ... I may have poured the entire bottle into it. My brother may have been a bit angry. But I was four, come on!)
b) the 'quality control' of freshly baked cookies.

There was always a way for me to get involved with cooking. Over the years, I learned the baking basics from my mum via her family recipe book, with lots of American, Italian and English recipes that had been passed down to her over the years. Overloaded with fresh produce from my dad's allotment all year round, I also learned how to cook simply with the seasons.

However, it wasn't until I was fifteen and finally discovered the wonderful world of food blogging that I really started to want to learn more about food. I couldn't believe that there were free (FREE!) recipes out there, countless in number with gorgeous images and such witty, creative minds behind them. It didn't take long for me to set up my own food blog, even though I had no clue whatsoever about what I was doing. I started out how most bloggers do: with an awkwardly designed, free website and the imminent pressure of naming it. After about a week of pondering, I decided on the URL and called my blog *Top With Cinnamon*, for two reasons, the first being that after giving my best friend a cinnamon-sugar topped blueberry muffin, she was equally enthused by and addicted to the topping as I was (the cinnamon-sugar crust remains my favourite part of any baked good). The second

reason was that I love to top things with cinnamon – coffee, cookies (have you ever tried a snickerdoodle cookie? They're awesome), muffins, scones. ALL GOOD. One thing I hadn't figured out yet was that when you say 'top with cinnamon' quickly to someone, they usually assume you said 'topped'. Most of the time, if people ask me what my blog is called and they repeat back to me, 'Oh, Topped With Cinnamon?' you'll probably see me do a wide-eyed, exhaley nose-laugh with a smile and nod because Google will inevitably correct them later. Then I internally slow-clap myself for being so great at naming things. Anyway, after that whole naming fiasco, I borrowed the family camera – a nice, chunky point-and-shoot with an amazing five megapixel sensor (it was 2011 and my phone didn't even have a camera on it) – and snuck around photographing food in awful lighting, probably with the camera flash on too.

It took about two weeks of this secret food photography for my mum to actually ask me if I had started a food blog, and for me to finally admit it. From then on, I couldn't stop. I kept on baking, cooking and photographing, encouraged and inspired by the amazing online foodie community. I've not only learned even more about food and photography, but made friends and met numerous incredible people.

One invaluable lesson I've also learned from blogging is the need for balance. When you're baking something (almost) every weekend, you've gotta find a way to justify the cake. Luckily, I'm not talking about just eating boring salads all through the week! It's easy to enjoy nourishing meals when you make them at home with simple recipes and when you're controlling the ingredients. This is essentially what you'll find in the pages of this book – from the wholesome and hearty to the downright indulgent, these are the recipes I love and live by, and hope you will too.

[CHAPTER ONE]

BREAKFAST + Brunch

CHOCOLATE + BANANA FRENCH TOAST

COURGETTE CORNBREAD PANCAKES (gluten-free)

COCONUT BERRY PANCAKES

10-MINUTE ALMOND GRANOLA (gluten-free with vegan options)

WHOLEMEAL HAND PIES (vegan)

CORNBREAD WITH CINNAMON-SUGAR

CRANBERRY FLAXSEED SCONES

PRETZEL CINNAMON ROLLS

BLUEBERRY SMOOTHIE

NO-BAKE CHOCOLATE GRANOLA COOKIES

WHOLEMEAL MAPLE PECAN BUNS

TRIPLE LEMON STREUSEL CAKE

BREAKFAST-Y BRUNCH foods have always been my favourite. I could (and sometimes do) eat them at any time of day. I love their not-too-sweet flavours and, of course, the excuse to eat fruity cake in the morning will never be complained about by me. There's something about that magical combination of a really good cup of coffee and a stack of pancakes that can immediately calm me down and make me excited all at the same time.

Mainly, though, I think it's really special to be able to just zone out at 10 a.m. on a Sunday morning and fully immerse yourself in making food you really love, which you eat right then and there. That's why I'm bringing you these recipes. Sure, they're not all for everyday eating (I don't think it's possible to live in a world where scones and streusel cake are a Monday to Sunday thing, without having to replace my entire wardrobe) but they're delicious and comforting to the max with a few healthy ingredient twists thrown in.

CHOCOLATE & BANANA
French Toast

[**SERVES 2-3**]

French toast has always been my favourite 'fancy' breakfast. There's cinnamon and maple syrup involved so it's a guaranteed winner. The problem is that I despise hovering by the stove, ridiculously hungry, waiting for the bread to cook. If I'm standing in the kitchen for more than ten minutes I'll probably end up eating a stray cookie sitting on the counter. Cue baked French toast: layer it all up in a pan and bake to crispy, gooey, melted perfection. It can even be made the night before and stored in the fridge before baking in the morning. Plus, I don't even have to be in the kitchen while it cooks, so I can avoid the previously mentioned cookie dilemma.

Ingredients

4 slices of bread, preferably stale

75 g (2½ oz/⅓ cup) Chocolate-Hazelnut Butter, store-bought or homemade (page 185)

1 egg

190 ml (6½ fl oz/¾ cup) milk

2 tbsp brown sugar

½ ripe banana, mashed

2 tbsp demerara (raw) sugar

Preparation

Preheat your oven to 180°C (350°F/Gas 4). Cut the bread into small cubes. Place half the cubes in a small baking dish and use a teaspoon to dot the bread with half of the chocolate-hazelnut butter. Cover with the rest of the bread cubes, then dot with the remaining chocolate-hazelnut butter.

In a small jug, combine the egg, milk, brown sugar and mashed banana with a fork. Pour over the bread, making sure you cover it all. At this point you can either cover the dish with plastic wrap and refrigerate it overnight, or bake straight away.

When you're ready to bake it, sprinkle with the demerara sugar and cook in the oven for 25–30 minutes, until it's puffy and crisp on top.

· COURGETTE ·
Cornbread Pancakes

[**MAKES 10 SMALL PANCAKES**]

* Gluten Free *

Growing up, the pancakes I ate were always made from a box-mix, which had been lovingly hauled back
in four-packs from infrequent visits to America. I don't think I realised I could make pancakes myself,
sans-mix, for a good ten years. Since then, I've been making pancakes very often for weekend breakfasts,
experimenting with different flours and add-ins to change the texture and flavour. These pancakes
have a slight crunch from the cornmeal and the courgette keeps them deliciously moist. You can also eliminate
the sugar to make a savoury pancake to serve with eggy brunch dishes.

Ingredients

100 g (3½ oz/½ cup) finely grated courgette
(zucchini)

55g (2 oz/½ cup) rolled oats

65 g (2¼ oz/½ cup) cornmeal

30 g (1 oz/¼ cup) ground almonds

1 tsp baking powder

¼ tsp bicarbonate of soda (baking soda)

2 tbsp granulated sugar (optional)

1 egg

190 ml (6½ fl oz/¾ cup) milk

sunflower oil, for frying

Preparation

Squeeze the grated courgette through a fine sieve to remove as much water as possible.

Place the oats, cornmeal, almonds, baking powder, bicarbonate of soda and sugar (if using) in a food processor and blitz until the oats are fine. Add the squeezed courgette, egg and milk and blend until well combined.

Heat about 2 teaspoons of oil in a large non-stick frying pan over a medium heat. Tilt and swirl the pan until it's evenly coated with oil. Spoon 2 tablespoons of batter into the pan to form each pancake (I usually cook 2 or 3 at a time, but it depends on the size of your pan). Cook the pancakes until bubbles form and burst on top, and the underside is golden. Flip over each pancake using a spatula and cook until golden on the other side. Repeat with the remaining batter, adding more oil to the pan as needed.

Note: Pancakes can be kept warm while you cook the remaining batter by placing them on a baking tray in an oven heated to 90°C (190°F/Gas ¼).

COCONUT BERRY
Pancakes

[MAKES 12 SMALL PANCAKES]

There's this little tradition between my mum and I. On the rare occasion that my dad isn't home for supper, we will have an evening meal of pancakes. (My dad would refuse to eat sweet pancakes for dinner, I'm sure.) I'm talking stacked-up, thick, fluffy pancakes. Of course there's maple syrup, sometimes a sprinkle of toasted pecans and a schmear of cream cheese (try it). These particular pancakes are some of the fluffiest I've ever made, thanks to the involvement of the ricotta. Oh, and don't worry if it sounds like something is going seriously wrong when you flip the pancake over — the berries may start to burst and will cause a hissing sound when the juice hits the pan.

Ingredients

60 g (2 oz/½ cup) wholemeal (whole-wheat) flour

95 g (3¼ oz/¾ cup) plain (all-purpose) flour

35 g (1 oz/⅓ cup) desiccated coconut

1 tsp baking powder

¼ tsp bicarbonate of soda (baking soda)

2 tbsp coconut sugar (or light brown sugar)

4 tbsp ricotta

190 ml (6½ fl oz/¾ cup) milk

1 egg

1 tsp vinegar or lemon juice

1 tbsp coconut oil or butter

vegetable or coconut oil, for frying

75 g (2½ oz/¾ cup) mixed berries
  (e.g. raspberries and redcurrants)

Preparation

In a medium jug, mix together the first 6 ingredients. Add the ricotta, milk, egg and vinegar and stir until just combined. Melt the coconut oil or butter in a large non-stick frying pan and then stir it into the batter.

Heat about 2 teaspoons of oil in the frying pan over a medium heat. Tilt and swirl the pan until it's evenly coated with oil. Spoon 2 tablespoons of batter into the pan to form each pancake — I usually cook 2 or 3 at a time, but it depends on the size of your pan. Sprinkle a few berries over each pancake. Cook the pancakes until bubbles form and burst on top, and the underside is golden. Flip over each pancake using a spatula and cook until golden on the other side. Repeat with the remaining batter, adding more oil to the pan as needed.

Note: Pancakes can be kept warm while you cook the remaining batter by placing them on a baking tray in an oven heated to 90°C (190°F/Gas ¼).

· 10–MINUTE ·
Almond Granola

[SERVES 2]

* Gluten-free with vegan options *

Granola is delicious. It's crunchy, toasty and fully customisable. Throw it on top of some yoghurt with fresh fruit – BAM! Breakfast or dessert. You can buy granola but making it is so much better, as it's guaranteed to be crisp and you can toss whatever the heck you want into the mixture. Usually granola is made by baking it, meaning you have to keep running back to the oven every few minutes to flip the mixture and rotate the pan to prevent burning. My stovetop version is so much easier and quicker to make. You just need a frying pan, wooden spoon and ten minutes to make it. Low commitment, high reward!

Ingredients

190 g (6⅔ oz/2 cups) rolled oats

35 g (1½ oz/¼ cup) almonds, roughly chopped

2 tbsp butter or coconut oil

3 tbsp honey, agave or maple syrup

Preparation

Dry-toast the oats and almonds together in a large deep frying pan over a high heat for 5 minutes, stirring often.

Make a hole in the middle of the mixture and add the butter or coconut oil along with the honey, agave or maple syrup. Continue to heat and stir the mixture for a further 5 minutes, making sure everything is well coated. Remove from the heat and allow to cool before transferring to a lidded jar for storage (it will keep for up to 2 weeks).

· WHOLEMEAL ·
Hand Pies

[**MAKES 10-12 PIES**]

* Vegan *
Can we eat pie for breakfast? Yes. Yes, we can when you can hold it in your hand.
Somehow downsizing pie to hand-held form makes this acceptable, but don't ask me how.
Just look at these pies and how breakfast-y they look. Yeah, whole-wheat crust, fruit, nut butter.
See, it's OK. Eat the pie.

Ingredients

1 quantity of *Wholemeal Pastry (page 178)*
1 quantity of filling (see below)
demerara (raw) sugar, for sprinkling

Apple-Chocolate-Hazelnut Filling
1 apple
1 tbsp lemon juice

75 g (2½ oz/5 tbsp) *Chocolate-Hazelnut Butter,*
store-bought or homemade (page 185)

Apricot-Almond Filling
180 g (6¼ oz/1 cup) dried apricots, roughly
chopped
75 g (2½ oz/5 tbsp) *Almond Butter, store-bought*
or homemade (page 190)

Preparation

Preheat the oven to 180°C (350°F/Gas 4) and line a baking tray with baking parchment.

To make the Apple-Chocolate-Hazelnut Filling
Peel, core and finely chop the apple. Toss in a bowl with the lemon juice and set aside.

To make the Apricot-Almond Filling
Bring the apricots and 250 ml (8½ fl oz/1 cup) water to the boil in a small saucepan. Reduce to a simmer, cover with a lid and cook for 15 minutes. Remove from the heat and set aside to cool.

On a lightly floured surface, roll out the pastry until it is 3 mm (⅛ in) thick. Cut out circles using a 7.5 cm (3 in) round cutter (or use an upturned 7.5 cm (3 in) bowl and cut around it with a sharp knife). Re-roll scraps as needed. You should end up with 20–24 circles.

To assemble, place a pastry circle on the lined baking tray. Dollop half a teaspoon of either the chocolate-hazelnut butter (for the apple pies) or the almond butter (for the apricot pies) in the centre of the circle. Top with a heaped teaspoon of the apple or apricot mixture accordingly.

Use your fingers to wet the edge of the pastry with some water, then top with a second circle of pastry. Pinch the edges together and crimp them with a fork to seal. Cut a small cross into the the top of the pastry (to let out the steam as it cooks), then brush with water and sprinkle with demerara sugar. Repeat with the remaining pastry circles and filling.

Bake for 17–20 minutes, until the edges are just browned and the juices are bubbling through the hole in the top of the pastry.

CORNBREAD WITH Cinnamon-Sugar

[**SERVES 6 GENEROUSLY**]

Every year my dad grows an incredible quantity of loganberries and raspberries – turning them into jam is his autumn tradition. You can always tell when there's a pot of jam being made from the scent of the fresh berries bubbling away on the stove, which drifts through the whole house. As do the expletives that are yelled when the jam inevitably boils over and burns, leaving a sticky mess everywhere. Yet somehow we still end up with a cellar of jars filled with the sweet-tart stuff. My dad's always giving the jam away to everyone, while I'm hiding jars so that there's enough for the rest of the year. I hoard it because around that time of year my mum makes cornbread. She'll divide it into six generous pieces and we'll eat it warm for breakfast. I like to halve it, spread on some Salted Treacle Butter (page 191), which melts in, before layering on plenty of berry jam.

Ingredients

2 tbsp salted butter

3 tbsp granulated sugar

1 egg

250 ml (8½ fl oz/1 cup) milk

110 g (3¾ oz/1 cup, minus 1 tbsp) cornmeal

110 g (3¾ oz/1 cup, minus 1 tbsp) plain (all-purpose) flour

1 tbsp, plus 2 tsp baking powder

Cinnamon-Sugar

2 tbsp granulated sugar

2 tsp ground cinnamon

Salted Treacle Butter (page 191) and jam, to serve

Preparation

Preheat the oven to 180°C (350°F/Gas 4). Butter a 20 cm (8 in) pie dish.

Melt the butter in a medium-sized pan, then take it off the heat and stir in the sugar, egg, milk and cornmeal. Add the flour and baking powder, stirring until just combined, then pour into the prepared pie dish.

Make the cinnamon-sugar by combining the sugar with the cinnamon in a small bowl. Sprinkle it over the surface of the batter. Bake for 25–30 minutes then serve warm with the salted treacle butter and jam.

· CRANBERRY ·
Flaxseed Scones

[MAKES 9]

Once in a while I'll buy one of those rustic sourdough loaves with pecans and dried cranberries
in it from the bakery in town. It is so good, especially toasted and spread with some salty, cultured butter.
Unfortunately, I have to make a twenty-minute tube journey to get this bread, and I'm not too
enthused about paying the transport fares. But nor am I keen on making my own sourdough culture at home.
Instead, I satisfy my cravings by making these cranberry scones with a crunchy sugar crust. I don't think
anyone would be disappointed with this trade-off. I'm certainly not.

Ingredients

250 g (9 oz/2 cups) plain (all-purpose) flour

4 tbsp ground flaxseed

2 tbsp granulated sugar

2 tsp baking powder

½ tsp salt

110 g (3¾ oz/½ cup) cold unsalted butter,
    cubed

80 g (2¾ oz/½ cup) dried cranberries

1 egg

125 ml (4 fl oz/½ cup) buttermilk,
    plus a little extra for brushing

50 g (2 oz/¼ cup) demerara (raw) sugar,
    for topping

Salted Treacle Butter (page 191), to serve

Preparation

Preheat the oven to 180°C (350°F/Gas 4). Line a baking tray with baking parchment.

Place the first 5 ingredients in a large bowl and stir together. Add the cubes of butter and use
your fingertips to rub them into the dry ingredients, leaving some pea-sized chunks of butter.
You'll have a moist, mealy mixture. Stir in the cranberries then make a well in the middle and
add the egg and buttermilk. Stir together until just combined.

Turn out the dough onto a lightly floured surface and knead it a few times, then roll it into a
square, 2 cm (¾ in) thick. Cut into 9 squares using a sharp knife, then transfer the squares to the
lined baking tray, placing them 2.5 cm (1 in) apart. Brush the tops of the scones with buttermilk
and sprinkle with demerara sugar. Bake for 25–30 minutes until browned and risen. Serve with
the salted treacle butter.

. PRETZEL .
Cinnamon Rolls

[MAKES 12]

Surprisingly, it took me a while to find out about cinnamon rolls. I don't think I knew about them until I was fourteen. Seriously, that is a shocking amount of time for someone who adores cinnamon as much as I do. Around the same time I also had one of those cinnamon-sugar-coated soft pretzels, after a pretzel stall opened in the mall near my school. It turns out that if you combine these two spiced, pillowy treats you make the ultimate cinnamon roll: a sticky swirl of cinnamon-layered dough with a dark, pretzely crust and sprinkle of chunky salt.

Ingredients

1 quantity of Basic Bread Dough (page 181) (made using 4 tbsp sugar)

100 g (3½ oz/½ cup) dark brown sugar

3 tbsp ground cinnamon

75 g (2½ oz/⅓ cup) unsalted butter, softened

1 tbsp bicarbonate of soda (baking soda)

Kosher salt, for sprinkling

Preparation

Grease a large, deep ovenproof dish with sunflower oil. On a lightly floured surface, roll the proved dough into a rectangle, 50 x 32 cm (20 x 12½ in).

Stir the sugar and cinnamon together in a bowl. Spread the butter over the surface of the dough and top with the cinnamon-sugar. Starting with a short edge, roll the dough into a 32 cm (12½ in) log, then cut the log into 12 even pieces and arrange each piece in the greased dish. Cover loosely with oiled plastic wrap and leave to rise in a warm place for 30 minutes. Preheat the oven to 180°C (350°F/Gas 4).

In a small bowl, stir together the bicarbonate of soda and 3 tablespoons of hot water. Remove the plastic wrap from the rolls and use a pastry brush to cover the rolls with the bicarbonate of soda mixture, then immediately sprinkle with salt. Bake for 35–45 minutes until dark brown and well risen.

. BLUEBERRY .
Smoothie

[**MAKES 1 LARGE GLASS OR 2 SMALL GLASSES**]

Let's just put it out there: smoothies can be amazingly delicious or TERRIBLE. When you buy
a smoothie it seems simple. 'It's just fruit, right? Yeah, I can totally make that.' No, no. It's not. I've found out
that there are some very bad combinations that can be made. Now that I've figured out this recipe
(which actually works and is super-refreshing) I don't need to keep trying weird combos and
subjecting my poor taste buds to my crazy experiments. The secret is in the apple juice: it provides the liquid
to let the mixture blend properly, and also sweetens it so that you don't need to add any sugar.
Note: You can blend in a handful of spinach leaves with the other smoothie ingredients if you're looking for
a nutritional boost. It doesn't change the flavour at all but will add some iron and more fibre.

Ingredients

125 g (4½ oz/1 cup) blueberries, fresh or frozen
a handful of raspberries, blackberries or grapes
1 banana, peeled

1 tbsp chia seeds (optional)
125 ml (4 fl oz/½ cup) cloudy apple juice
a handful of ice

Preparation

Blitz all the ingredients in a blender until smooth. Serve immediately.

For easy morning prep, place the berries, chopped banana and chia seeds in a sandwich
bag and freeze. That way you just have to blend the contents of the sandwich bag with the
apple juice and ice for a really quick breakfast.

NO-BAKE CHOCOLATE
Granola Cookies

[MAKES 7 LARGE COOKIES]

My alarm goes off at 6.45 a.m. Then the subsequent ones at 7 a.m., 7.15 a.m. and 7.20 a.m.
to wake me up for school. As the winter months approach it's (for some reason) even harder to have the
motivation to get up, so there are some days when I open my eyes and it's a quarter to eight.
Needless to say, I have to rush to get out of the door. There's definitely no time to make my carefully layered
toast (with nut butter, honey and sliced fruit) or yoghurt and muesli, let alone enough time to eat them.
That's when things like granola bars (or cookies in this case) come in handy. I can grab one on my
way out of the door for some no-fuss morning fuel.

Ingredients

70g (2¼ oz/¾ cup) rolled oats

90g (3 oz/½ cup) pitted dates

35 g (1 oz/¼ cup) almonds

2 tbsp Almond Butter, store-bought
or homemade (page 190)

1 tbsp maple syrup

1 tbsp cocoa powder

30g (1 oz/1 cup) cornflakes or puffed rice cereal

30g (1 oz) dark (bittersweet) chocolate
(minimum 60% cocoa solids), melted (optional)

Preparation

Line a baking tray with baking parchment. Dry-toast the oats in a large frying pan over a high heat,
stirring often, until fragrant. Remove from the heat and leave to cool in the pan.

In a food processor, blend the dates, almonds, almond nut butter, maple syrup, 2 tablespoons of
water and the cocoa powder until a paste is formed. Add the paste to the oats with the cornflakes
and knead together gently with your hands. Divide into 7 balls and flatten them slightly onto the
lined baking tray. Drizzle with the chocolate (if using) and leave to set at room temperature.

WHOLEMEAL MAPLE Pecan Buns

[MAKES 12]

There are certain flavours in the world that were meant for each other, with maple syrup and toasted pecans being my ultimate food couple. If they were celebrities I would be rooting for MapeCan (their couple name, obviously) forever. However, they are ingredients so instead of stalking gossip mags, I stalk cookbooks, scouring recipe indexes for any mention of maple-pecan. Don't even get me started on those Danish pastry plaits that are filled with a maple filling and sprinkled with toasted pecans. It's a good thing that they're a lot of effort to make, otherwise I'd be eating them 24/7. I took inspiration from them here though, topping spheres of bread dough with spoonfuls of maple-pecan pie filling and a sprinkling of salt. It's sticky bun meets Danish plait meets pecan pie. Utterly fabulous (especially if you whip up some Salted Treacle Butter to spread on the hot rolls, too, see page 191).

Ingredients

125 ml (4 fl oz/½ cup) maple syrup
2 tbsp demerara (raw) sugar
1 tsp unsalted butter
¼ tsp salt
2 tbsp milk
95 g (3¼ oz/⅔ cup) chopped pecans, plus
    12 pecan halves, to serve

1 quantity of Basic Bread Dough (page 181)
    (made using half wholemeal/whole-wheat
    flour and 4 tbsp sugar and left to rise for
    1 hour)
flaky salt, for sprinkling
Salted Treacle Butter (page 191), to serve

Preparation

Liberally butter a 12-cup muffin tin. In a small saucepan, heat the maple syrup, sugar, butter, salt and milk over a medium-low heat, stirring gently, until melted and combined. Bring to a simmer then remove from the heat. Divide the pecans and the maple mixture between the cups of the buttered muffin tin.

Punch down the bread dough and divide it into 12 balls then place a ball of dough in each muffin cup. Cover with oiled plastic wrap and leave to rise in a warm place for 30–45 minutes, until

doubled in size. Preheat the oven to 180°C (350°F/Gas 4).

Once the buns have risen, remove the plastic wrap and bake them for 20–25 minutes until puffed and golden brown. Immediately flip the hot tin upside down onto a cooling rack and leave for 5 minutes. Lift up the muffin tin and scrape out any of the maple topping that may be stuck, placing it on top of the buns. Top each bun with a pecan half and a sprinkle of flaky salt. Serve warm with the salted treacle butter.

TRIPLE LEMON
Streusel Cake

[SERVES 12]

When I want lemon in a baked good I. Seriously. Want. Lemon. I've been known to make extra lemon glaze and double-dip poppy seed muffins in it just to make sure there's enough tang going on. In this cake I've layered a lemony cake batter with a tangy lemon-cream cheese ribbon and drizzled it with a lemon glaze. Is that enough lemon for me? Well just about, but don't judge me if I tell you that I ate a slice with extra lemon curd.

Ingredients

The Topping

2 tbsp demerara (raw) sugar
30 g (1 oz/¼ cup) plain (all-purpose) flour
2 tbsp rolled oats
2 tbsp unsalted butter

The Cake

110 g (3¾ oz/½ cup) unsalted butter
150 g (5 oz/¾ cup) granulated sugar
1 tbsp lemon zest
2 tbsp lemon juice
160 ml (5½ fl oz/⅔ cup) buttermilk

2 eggs
150 g (5 fl oz/1¼ cups) plain (all-purpose) flour
2 tsp baking powder
½ tsp salt
60 g (2 oz/⅔ cup) rolled oats
75 g (2½ oz/5 tbsp) cream cheese
  or crème fraîche
4 tbsp lemon curd

The Glaze

70 g (2½ oz/⅔ cup) icing (confectioners') sugar
1 tbsp lemon juice

Preparation

Combine the topping ingredients in a medium bowl, rubbing the butter into the dry ingredients until a crumbly texture is achieved. Set aside.

Preheat the oven to 180°C (350°F/ Gas 4). Grease and flour a 20 cm (8-inch) square cake tin.

Make the cake batter: melt the butter in a large pan over a low heat. Remove the pan from the heat and stir in the sugar, lemon zest and juice and the buttermilk. Beat in the eggs then stir in the flour, baking powder, salt and oats until well combined (the oats

will make it lumpy, so it won't be perfectly smooth). Spread a third of the batter into the prepared cake tin. Stir together the cream cheese and lemon curd and spread this over surface of the batter. Dollop the remaining batter on top of the lemon curd layer and spread it out evenly. Cover with the topping and bake for 35–45 minutes until a toothpick inserted into the centre of the cake comes out clean.

Combine the glaze ingredients and drizzle this over the cake with a spoon.

CHAPTER TWO

. SIDES .

TASTY PITTA CHIPS

CHICKPEA + POMEGRANATE DIP

CHUNKY GUACAMOLE

GREEN BEANS WITH TOMATO + RED ONION

RICOTTA ASPARAGUS FRITTERS

SQUASH, FETA + SAGE FOCACCIA

PEACH + TOMATO SALSA

COURGETTE 'SPAGHETTI' WITH CHILLI

ROASTED CAULIFLOWER

SWEET + SPICY ROASTED CHICKPEAS (vegan, gluten-free)

STROMBOLI (ISH)

FIG + WALNUT PARMESAN CRACKERS

BAKED ROSEMARY POLENTA CHIPS

SIDES ARE akin to bonus points for a meal. You've got a lasagne (score!) but also, hey, look, a side of some kind of garlicky courgettes! You've got soup, but woah: check out this focaccia, man. They're the equivalent of pic-n-mix for the savoury world: pair a couple of sides together, then add a fried egg or some grilled meat and you've got yourself a simple, satisfying meal. Alternatively you can take them down the starter or dinner-party-snack route because they are awesome for sharing. If you're me, there's also the hidden agenda of eating most of them yourself in lieu of an actual meal. They are essentially everything I could want for sustenance: warm and filling, often spiked with garlic, jalapeño or cheese. It's the kind of food that I will want to eat no matter what, especially if there is evening light, the company of great friends, plus a pack of playing cards (the only situation in which I'll actually play card games) or alone with a good magazine.

.TASTY PITTA. *Chips*

[**SERVES 4-6**]

Cross a crisp and a breadstick and what do you get? Pitta chips. They're pretty much fail-safe, impressive and addictive. You can make mega batches with minimum effort for when you have more than a few people round. Don't like Italian herbs? That's fine! Sprinkle on smoky paprika, cayenne pepper and ground coriander, or maybe just rub each pitta half with a garlic clove before cutting into strips. These pitta chips will happily scoop up any of the dips on the following pages.

Not-so-secret tip: sprinkle on some cinnamon-sugar instead for a sweet version.

Ingredients

3 wholemeal (whole-wheat) pitta breads

2 tbsp olive oil

1 tsp dried mixed herbs

   (e.g. thyme, basil and oregano)

a few sprigs of fresh thyme (optional)

a generous pinch each of salt and freshly ground

   black pepper

Preparation

Preheat the oven to 180°C (350°F/Gas 4). Toast the pitta breads in a toaster until they just puff up (you'll need to turn them around so each end gets toasted).

Cut along the edge of each toasted pitta bread to split it in half and then cut each half into 16 strips. Place on a baking tray and drizzle with the oil. Sprinkle with the herbs, salt and pepper. Bake for 3–5 minutes until just crisp and slightly browned

CHICKPEA & Pomegranate Dip

[SERVES 4]

Even if you don't like chickpeas you will love this dip. Everyone loves this dip. My brother and I have been known to demolish the whole batch between us in a very short space of time. Actually, if you make this, please make a double batch – you'll need it. Pomegranate molasses may seem like a gourmet ingredient if you've never heard of it before but you can now find it in most supermarkets. If you really can't get a hold of some, replace it with a balsamic glaze (either bought or made by slowly reducing balsamic vinegar and a little sugar in a saucepan over a low heat until thick) or balsamic vinegar mixed with 1 teaspoon of granulated sugar. The Tasty Pitta Chips (page 45) are perfect for serving with this dip.

Ingredients

400g (14 oz) can chickpeas (garbanzo beans), drained and rinsed

4 tbsp olive oil

1 tbsp pomegranate molasses, plus more to serve

½ tsp flaky salt

a generous pinch of freshly ground black pepper

1 tsp cumin seeds

2 jalapeños, de-seeded and finely chopped

1 small red onion, peeled and finely chopped

3 tbsp fresh coriander (cilantro), roughly chopped

3 tbsp fresh mint, roughly chopped

100 g (3½ oz/½ cup) feta, crumbled

a handful of pomegranate seeds

Preparation

Place the chickpeas, oil, pomegranate molasses, salt and pepper in a blender and pulse briefly until combined but still slightly chunky (alternatively place them in a large bowl and mash using a potato masher or fork).

Transfer to a bowl and stir in the rest of the ingredients, reserving a little feta and some of the pomegranate seeds. Drizzle with extra pomegranate molasses and serve with the reserved pomegranate seeds and feta scattered on top.

. CHUNKY .
Guacamole

[SERVES 4]

I am a bit of a latecomer to the avocado scene, as I used to think I didn't like the flavour. It was probably due to stubbornness and from not trying it in delicious dip form! Guacamole or 'guac' as (far too often) I refer to it, is what converted me and is now a favourite. Given the opportunity, I would eat it with tortilla chips as a main meal. Just put a bowl of it within a ten-metre radius of me and you'll have yourself a gauc-homing Izy. Don't worry though, I'd totally help you make more and I'd taste-test it multiple times to make sure it's OK.

Note: You can add a splash of gin or tequila to your guac for an extra kick!

Ingredients

4 ripe avocados

5–6 ripe cherry tomatoes, finely diced

1 small red onion or shallot, peeled
  and finely chopped

½ tsp flaky salt, plus more to taste

3 splashes of hot sauce

a large handful of fresh coriander (cilantro),
  roughly chopped, plus whole leaves to garnish

juice of 1 or 2 limes, to taste

lemon wedges, to serve

Preparation

Cut the avocados in half and tap each stone with a sharp knife, then twist and lift up to remove. Scoop the avocado flesh into a medium-sized bowl.

Add the tomatoes, onion, salt, hot sauce and coriander, then use a fork to gently mash the mixture together, adding lime juice and more salt to taste. Keep mashing until the desired consistency is reached. Garnish with a few coriander leaves and serve with wedges of lemon. This goes great with some Tasty Pitta Chips (page 45) — perfect for dunking!

GREEN BEANS WITH
Tomato + Red Onion

[SERVES 4-6]

In the summer months my dad brings panniers of green beans back from the allotment.
At first they're perfectly fine cooked simply and sprinkled with flaky salt, but after a month of this it has gone
on long enough. To make them interesting to eat again, they get cooked up with tomatoes (fresh
ones if they're around) and sweet red onion. It's impossible to stop eating them when they're served like this,
but if you want, you can fry up some pancetta or bacon with the garlic and onion for extra flavour.

Ingredients

500g (1 lb 2 oz) green beans, trimmed
   (you can use a mixture of runner and
   French beans)
2 red onions, peeled and finely diced
2 garlic cloves, peeled and minced
2 tbsp olive oil

5 medium tomatoes, roughly chopped,
   or 400g (14 oz) can chopped tomatoes
2 tbsp apple cider vinegar
1 tsp granulated sugar
½ tsp salt

Preparation

Cut the beans into roughly 5 cm lengths and cook them in a large pot of salted boiling water for
5 minutes, then drain.

Sauté the onions and garlic with the oil in a large frying pan over a medium heat until the onions
are soft. Add the tomatoes, vinegar, sugar and salt. Cook for 5 minutes over a medium heat, then
add the beans and stir to combine. Leave to cook for a further 5 minutes then pour into a large bowl
and serve.

RICOTTA ASPARAGUS Fritters

[SERVES 4]

This was previously a 'no-recipe' recipe that my mum had stored in the recipe book called her brain. We hadn't made it in a while so I had to ask her what the measurements were and in her true mum-like way, she just wrote down some ambiguous things like 'around half a tub of ricotta' and 'breadcrumbs' on a scrap of paper. 'What about the Parmesan, ma?' 'Oh yeah, but just a bit. The main part of the batter is the ricotta!' With those rough guidelines I made them, filling in the gaps where I could. As asparagus is one of my favourite spring vegetables, I was ALL OVER these. They're great served with grilled meat but they're fine as a main course too, if you serve them with a side of grain salad or crusty bread.

Ingredients

4 eggs

125 g (4½ oz/½ cup plus 1 tbsp) ricotta

2 tbsp grated Parmesan, plus extra shavings
   to serve

¼ tsp salt

80 g (2¾ oz/½ cup) fine dried breadcrumbs

20 thick or 30 thin asparagus spears,
   woody ends removed (top tip: bend each
   stalk until it snaps)

vegetable oil, for frying

Preparation

In a jug, whisk together the eggs, ricotta, Parmesan, salt and breadcrumbs. Leave to sit while you prepare the asparagus.

Half-fill a deep frying pan with water, add the asparagus and place over a medium heat. Once the water has started to boil, cook for 4 minutes until the asparagus is just tender. Drain the water from the pan and set the asparagus to one side. Dry the pan.

In the same pan, heat 2 tablespoons of oil over a medium heat. Dollop a heaped tablespoon of the batter into the pan and top with 2 thick or 3 thin spears of asparagus. Top with a little extra batter (about 1 teaspoon) to seal the asparagus into the fritter. Cook for 3 minutes until golden brown, then flip over the fritter and cook until golden brown on the other side. Transfer to a plate lined with paper towels, then repeat with the rest of the batter and asparagus. Serve the fritters with Parmesan shavings scattered on top.

. SQUASH, FETA .
+ Sage Focaccia

[**SERVES 4-6**]

Focaccia is like an excuse to eat pizza with extra bread and a dipping bowl of balsamic-puddled
olive oil while calling it a 'side'. Normally you'll find it sprinkled with rosemary and coarse sea salt.
Occasionally, some sun-dried tomatoes or olives may make an appearance. That is what I
call a luxury focaccia, like the ones I've bought from artisanal bakeries after a day of shopping. I share
it with my friends, ripping hunks of bread warm from the bag while sitting on the bus home.
Yeah, we're probably being judged/secret-envy-eyed by everyone else but do you know how hard it
is to hold a loaf of warm bread and not tear into it? Extremely. So I think the bus people understand.
Here, the chewy loaf is topped with cheese, squash and sage for a comforting, autumnal flavour.
It's great eaten alongside soup or a light stew.

Ingredients

1 quantity of No-Knead Flatbread Dough
   (page 179) (let it rise for at least 2 hours)
½ small butternut squash, peeled and de-seeded
50 g (2 oz/¼ cup) ricotta
50 g (2 oz/¼ cup) feta, crumbled

a small handful of rocket (arugula) leaves
4–6 fresh sage leaves
2 tbsp olive oil
½ tsp coarse salt

Preparation

Knock back the dough and place it in a well-oiled 25 x 18 cm (10 x 7 in), or 20 cm (8 in) square
baking tin. Leave it in a warm place to rise for another 30 minutes.

Preheat the oven to 200°C (400°F/Gas 6). Finely slice the butternut squash. In a small bowl,
stir together the ricotta and feta.

Use your fingers to push dimples into the surface of the risen dough, then dot the ricotta and
feta mixture over the top. Cover with the butternut squash and rocket then rip the sage leaves
over the top. Drizzle with the oil and sprinkle with the salt. Bake for 30–40 minutes until risen and
golden brown. Turn out onto a wire rack and leave to cool. Once cooled, cut into big squares or
rectangles with a large serrated knife and serve.

PEACH & TOMATO Salsa

[SERVES 2-4]

Besides from being a sassy dance, salsa is also a very general term for a mixture of finely chopped vegetables. I've seen corn salsa, pineapple salsa, cucumber salsa, hot salsas, cold salsas, chunky and smooth. So if you ask me what salsa is, I'll probably just start dancing at you instead of revealing that I'm not actually too sure of the definition. This recipe is closest to a basic cold tomato salsa but I've amped it up with peaches and basil. You can leave it chunky, as I have, or blitz it with a hand-held blender for a smoother, more sauce-like situation.

Ingredients

2 peaches, stones removed, roughly chopped

10 cherry tomatoes, roughly chopped

1 lime

2 tbsp roughly chopped fresh basil

3 splashes of hot sauce

1 tbsp agave syrup

¼ tsp salt

Preparation

Place the peaches and tomatoes in a bowl, leaving behind as much juice as possible. Zest the lime straight into the bowl, then cut the lime in half and add the juice of one half. Add the basil, hot sauce and agave, season with the salt and stir together.

· COURGETTE ·
'Spaghetti' with Chilli

[SERVES 2-4]

There are a few things that grow extremely well in the British climate, a surprising one being courgettes, thus there's always an over-abundance of them. Apart from grilling or roasting them, frying them in garlic and olive oil is a family favourite. They're incredibly creamy and sweet when you get them right. Shredding the courgettes on a box grater gives you ribbony noodles which are awesome as a side dish or mixed in with spaghetti to bulk it up a bit, or served simply with a little grated Parmesan. They're also good for the days when you've eaten way too much bread to be justifiable but still want a massive bowl of faux spaghetti with tomato sauce for supper.

Ingredients

2 large courgettes (zucchini)

1 tbsp olive oil

2 garlic cloves, peeled and minced or grated

¼ tsp salt, or to taste

a large pinch of dried chilli flakes

grated Parmesan, to serve (optional)

Preparation

Cut the ends off the courgettes. Take a box grater and lay it on its side so that the side with the largest holes is facing upwards. Push the courgette along the top of the box grater in long strokes to create ribbony shreds. Continue until all the courgette has been grated into ribbons. If you don't have a box grater, use a peeler to peel the courgettes into wide ribbons, then stack the wide ribbons on top of each other and slice them in half lengthways to make them thinner.

Heat the oil with the garlic in a large frying pan over a medium heat, adding the courgette, salt and dried chilli flakes. Sauté for 5 minutes until the courgette is slightly tender. Serve immediately with the Parmesan on top, if using.

. ROASTED .
Cauliflower

[**SERVES 2-4**]

I used to not like cauliflower. It's hard to know what to do with it apart from boil it and serve it plain, which I find can make it bitter and pretty boring. I'm secretly happy that most people, in my experience, don't like cauliflower either. It means that it's pretty cheap to buy so I can make A LOT of roasted cauliflower, on the regular. Roasting it imparts a tenderness, with a creamy and slightly sweet flavour. I'm completely smitten with it and it goes with pretty much everything! You can of course switch around the flavourings: season it with smoked paprika or curry powder pre-bake, or toss it with a mustard vinaigrette once roasted.

Note: Roast the cauliflower with some pancetta for even more flavour.

Ingredients

1 large cauliflower, outer leaves and stalk
    removed
2 tbsp olive oil
½ tsp garlic salt

¼ tsp freshly ground black pepper
½ tsp dried thyme or a few sprigs of fresh thyme
    (optional)

Preparation

Preheat the oven to 180°C (350°F/Gas 4). Split the cauliflower into florets then slice the florets into quarters or thirds and place them on a baking tray.

Drizzle with the oil and sprinkle with the garlic salt, pepper and thyme, if using. Use your hands to toss the cauliflower until it is evenly coated then bake for 30 minutes until golden brown.

SWEET & SPICY Roasted Chickpeas

[SERVES 4]

* Vegan, gluten-free *

Snacking could probably be my main profession. I am a pro at finding little snacky things to ruin my appetite – it's a curse and a blessing, I guess. Tossing chickpeas in a marinade and roasting them happens to be one of the best, most easily consumable snacks around. I mean, you usually wouldn't eat a whole can of chickpeas yourself just off the bat. But if they're roasted and glistening I will attack them mercilessly. They happily make a perfect accompaniment to main dishes too, so sometimes I will use my willpower to hold off on the chickpea attack so I can save them for mealtimes.

Ingredients

400 g (14 oz) can chickpeas (garbanzo beans), drained and rinsed

1 tbsp soy sauce (gluten-free)

1 tbsp white wine vinegar

1 tbsp dark brown or cane sugar

1 tbsp sweet chilli sauce

½ tsp Sriracha or hot sauce

1 tbsp toasted sesame oil

Preparation

Preheat the oven to 200°C (400°F/Gas 6). Put the chickpeas in a bowl with all the other ingredients and stir until coated. Tip them onto a large baking tray and spread them out in a single layer. Bake for 5 minutes, then remove the tray from the oven and give it a shake. Bake for another 10 minutes, then remove, shake again, and bake for a final 5 minutes. Cool before serving.

. STROMBOLI .
(ish)

[**MAKES 1 LARGE LOAF OR 2 MEDIUM LOAVES**   ]

Stromboli is usually just a rectangle of dough covered with cheese and some cured meat then
rolled up and baked as a log. I do this, but I put it into a loaf pan before baking it
(hence the 'ish' in the name). No one will criticise you for doing this, don't worry. Not when there's
warm bread swirled with melted cheese, basil and meat sitting in front of their face.
They'll be too busy eating all of the bread to say anything.

Ingredients

1 quantity of Basic Bread Dough (page 181)
(let it rise for 1 hour until doubled in size)
75 g (2½ oz) prosciutto, Parma or
Serrano ham

125 g (4½ oz) mozzarella, finely chopped
or grated
125 g (4½ oz) provolone or Cheddar, grated
a large handful of torn fresh basil

Preparation

Grease a large (30 cm/12 in) loaf tin or 2 medium (20 cm/8 in) loaf tins with sunflower oil.

On a lightly floured surface, roll out the dough into a 40 cm (16 in) square. Cover evenly with the
ham, cheeses and basil. Tightly roll the dough into a log and trim off the ends.

If you're using a large loaf tin, lift the dough into the tin, placing it seam-side down. If you're
using medium loaf tins, cut the log in half to make 2 shorter logs and place each one in a loaf tin,
seam-side down. Cover with oiled plastic wrap and leave the dough to rise for 20 minutes while
you preheat the oven to 180°C (350°F/Gas 4).

Bake the large loaf for 40–50 minutes and the smaller loaves for 25–35 minutes. They should be
risen and well browned on top. Leave for 10 minutes before turning out onto a cutting board. Slice
thickly and serve warm.

FIG & WALNUT
Parmesan Crackers

[MAKES AROUND 40 CRACKERS]

Fancy crackers! Fancy crackers! You'll impress anyone with these, even though they're easier to make than usual crackers. No flouring surfaces. No rolling dough so thin that it sticks to the counter. No having to leave the kitchen because you're too annoyed to scrape up the dough and re-roll it. Bake in a loaf pan, freeze, slice and toast. Simple.

Ingredients

170 g (6 oz/1⅓ cup) wholemeal
   (whole-wheat) flour
65 g (2¼ oz/½ cup) buckwheat flour
1 tsp baking powder
1 tsp bicarbonate of soda (baking soda)
50 g (2 oz/½ cup) Parmesan, finely grated

¼ tsp salt
5 tbsp honey or agave syrup
60 g (2 oz/½ cup) walnuts, roughly chopped
60 g (2 oz/½ cup) pumpkin seeds
150 g (5 oz/½ cup) dried figs, roughly chopped

Preparation

Preheat the oven to 160°C (300°F/Gas 2). Grease two 8 x 18 cm (3 x 7 in) loaf tins with butter. In a large bowl, stir together the first 6 ingredients. Add 375ml (12½ fl oz) water and the honey and stir until well combined. Stir in the walnuts, pumpkin seeds and dried figs. Divide the batter between the loaf tins and bake for 40–50 minutes, until the edges have started to shrink away from the tins and the loaves are dark on top. Leave to cool on a wired rack and then wrap in plastic wrap and freeze for at least 3–4 hours.

Preheat the oven to 160°C (300°F/Gas 2). Unwrap and thinly slice the frozen loaves into roughly 3 mm (1/8 in) thick slices. Allow them to thaw a little then place the slices on a baking tray lined with baking parchment and bake for 10–15 minutes. Let them cool on a wire rack — the crackers will crisp as they cool. You can store them in an airtight container for up to a week. (If they start to soften, just pop them back into the oven at 160°C (300°F/Gas 2) for a few minutes.)

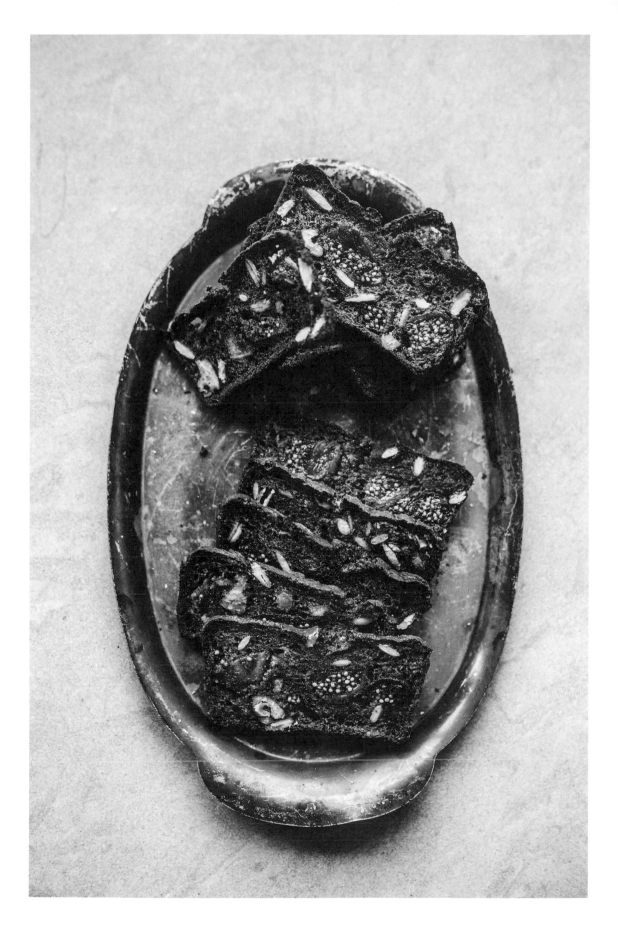

·BAKED ROSEMARY·
Polenta Chips

[**MAKES ABOUT 20 CHIPS**]

Polenta chips are for the times when you want to make oven fries but don't have any potatoes. They aren't a replacement for potatoes; don't worry friends, I'm not trying to remove the beloved chip from your life. They are, however, much more exciting in terms of texture and flavour potential. Take a regular fry: what can you do? You can season it with spices or herbs. That's about it. Take a polenta chip, however, and you have access to the actual 'meat' so to speak, of the chip. You can mix different cheeses or purées into the polenta while you cook it (sweet potato polenta is major) and also get whatever herbs or spices you want in there. You then get the opportunity to season the outer layer, too. Double flavour layers call for double exclamation marks!! I've gone and put garlic, ricotta and Parmesan IN the polenta, and then rosemary and truffle salt ON it. What results is the perfect harmony of mega flavour and cheesy, soft centre encased by a crisp outer layer.

Ingredients

125 ml (4 fl oz/½ cup) milk

1 clove of garlic, peeled and minced

160 g (5½ oz/1 cup) dry polenta

1 tbsp unsalted butter

100 g (3½ oz/½ cup) ricotta

2 tbsp grated Parmesan

a large pinch of salt

1 tsp dried rosemary

a large pinch of truffle salt or regular salt

1 tbsp vegetable oil

Preparation

In a large pan bring 500 ml (17 fl oz/ 2 cups) water, the milk and the garlic to the boil over a medium heat. Gradually add the polenta, while stirring, until thickened (it can take anywhere between 5 and 15 minutes). Then stir in the butter, ricotta, Parmesan and salt.

Spread the mixture on a foil-lined baking tray in a layer roughly 1 cm (1½ in) thick. Sprinkle with the rosemary and salt, pressing it gently into the surface with your hands. Chill until set, roughly 30 minutes to 1 hour.

Preheat the oven to 200°C (400°F/Gas 6). Once set, cut the polenta into 1 cm (1½ in) wide strips. Grease the lined baking tray with a little oil and then spread the polenta chips on top. Drizzle or spray the chips with oil too, and bake for 20–30 minutes, until golden brown, flipping them over halfway through the baking time.

CHAPTER THREE

. MAINS .

HALLOUMI, QUINOA + POMEGRANATE SALAD

SWEET POTATO + SHREDDED BEEF CHILLI

PRAWN + CORN SOUP

UDON NOODLE + MUSHROOM SOUP

CRISPY AUBERGINE WITH KALE PESTO FETTUCCINE

ROASTED VEGETABLE + PESTO GALETTE

PORK RAGÙ WITH AUBERGINE + PAPPARDELLE

GRIDDLED CHICKEN SALAD

CHICKEN TACOS WITH PEACH BBQ SAUCE

SQUASH, PANCETTA + CAULIFLOWER RISOTTO

SWEET + STICKY PORK

TUNA SALAD WITH BLACKENED TOMATOES

TOMATO SOUP WITH GARLIC + PIZZETTE

CARAMELISED ONION, THYME + BEAN POT PIES

WHILE MOST of the time I really enjoy cooking and find
it a way to relax and be creative, it can be an extremely
stressful situation. For me, there are a few factors which
can cause that to happen: people I don't know watching
me while I cook, time pressure or cooking dinner for more
than six people. It's not often that these things happen
but when they do I will go into meltdown mode and will
inevitably burn the food or my hands, mix up tablespoons
with teaspoons and just generally become a messy-bunned,
hot mess. Thankfully, when I cook a main meal, I'm usually
only feeding myself or four people so I can avoid the
stress-bomb problem. There have been some times when
mass cooking has gone well and that is usually when I've
got a recipe that needs minimal hands-on time (like slow-
cooked meat or big pots of soup). For these reasons, the
recipes in this chapter are small-scale the majority of the
time, but there are a few that can easily serve a flock of
hungry people or be doubled or tripled to accommodate
more mouths without a load of extra work. Hopefully I'll
remember to take my own advice and make these kinds
of dishes for mass-catering, rather than attempt to serve
things like pizza (in what world would that be a good idea?
I just don't know).

HALLOUMI, QUINOA · Pomegranate Salad

[SERVES 4]

If you're not eating halloumi you're not living right. It's one of the BEST goat/sheep's milk cheeses, in my opinion. Whenever I see it mentioned on a menu I will be ordering that dish, no doubt. It's salty and chewy with a crisp, toasted outer layer, which makes it impossible not to love. In this recipe we bake it into golden layers and crumble it over a slightly sweet quinoa salad. Yeah, quinoa: the grain (well, actually it's a seed if we're getting technical) you always hear people talking about in the supermarket because 'It's sooo good for you'. It's also a deliciously nutty source of starch, protein and fibre and pairs really well with the crunch of the pomegranate seeds and pine nuts.

Ingredients

170 g (6 oz/1 cup) quinoa, rinsed thoroughly
¾ tsp salt
250 g (9 oz) halloumi
1 small red onion, peeled and finely sliced
50 g (2 oz/⅓ cup) raisins
50 g (2 oz/¼ cup) pine nuts (pine kernels),
    lightly toasted
a large handful of fresh coriander (cilantro),
    roughly chopped
a large handful of pomegranate seeds

Lime-Pomegranate Dressing

juice of 1 lime
1 tbsp granulated sugar
2 tbsp pomegranate molasses (if you don't have
    any use balsamic vinegar, balsamic glaze,
    or apple cider vinegar)
3 tbsp vegetable oil
a large pinch of salt

Preparation

Put the quinoa in a medium, lidded pot with 500ml (17 fl oz/2 cups) boiling water and the salt. Cook over a medium heat for 15 minutes until all the water has been absorbed. Remove from the heat, fluff with a fork and set aside to cool.

While the quinoa cooks, slice the halloumi into roughly 5 mm (¼ in) thick slices and place on a foil-lined baking tray. Cook under the grill for 3–4 minutes, until golden. Flip over the cheese and scatter the sliced red onion onto the tray. Grill again until the other side of the cheese is golden. Remove the cheese from the grill and let it cool before breaking it into smaller pieces. Allow the onions to cook for a few minutes longer.

Shake the dressing ingredients together in a lidded jar until emulsified. Stir half of the dressing into the quinoa along with the onions, raisins, pine nuts and coriander. Transfer to a platter. Scatter the halloumi and pomegranate seeds over, then drizzle the rest of the dressing over and serve.

SWEET POTATO & Shredded Beef Chilli

[SERVES 8-10]

When it comes to serving a lot of people, chilli is a MIRACLE dish. You throw all the ingredients into a cast iron pot and leave them to cook down into a tender, flavourful and filling stew. The secret ingredient here is time. It's a game changer — letting the beef take on a melting texture and leaving the ingredients to meld into a luscious sauce you won't be able to stop eating. Serve it over rice or quinoa, or wrap it up with some Chunky Guac (page 48) and sour cream in a soft tortilla.

Ingredients

2 tbsp brown sugar

1 tsp salt

¼ tsp ground cloves

2 tsp ground cinnamon

1 tsp smoked paprika

1 tsp ground cumin

1 tsp dried oregano

1 tsp dried thyme or 1 tsp fresh thyme leaves

1 tsp ground cayenne (add to taste)

800 g (1 lb 12 oz) beef
(braising steak or brisket)

2 onions, peeled and sliced

1 tbsp olive oil

2 garlic cloves, peeled and minced or grated

3 x 400 g (14 oz) cans chopped tomatoes

500 ml (17 fl oz/2 cups) beer

2 tbsp apple cider vinegar

3 sweet potatoes, peeled

400 g (14 oz) can kidney beans, drained
and rinsed

2 (bell) peppers, de-seeded and sliced into strips

To serve: sour cream (or plain yoghurt), fresh
coriander (cilantro), lime wedges, cooked rice,
quinoa or tortilla chips

Preparation

Preheat the oven to 160°C (300°F/Gas 2). Mix together the sugar, salt, cloves, cinnamon, paprika, cumin, oregano, thyme and cayenne in a bowl. Rub all over the beef and set aside.

In a large ovenproof pan with a lid, sauté the onions in the oil over a medium heat until translucent. Add the garlic and cook for 1 minute, then stir in the tomatoes, 250 ml (8½ fl oz) water, the beer and the vinegar. Add the beef to the pan, cover with the lid, place in the oven and leave to cook for 2 hours.

Cut the peeled sweet potatoes into roughly 2.5 cm (1 in) chunks. Uncover the pan and add the sweet potatoes, beans and peppers. Cover with the lid again and return to the oven for a further hour. When ready to serve, shred the meat in the pot using two forks, and stir it into the sauce. Serve with sour cream, chopped coriander, lime wedges and rice, quinoa or tortilla chips.

PRAWN &
Corn Soup

[SERVES 3-4]

I'm pretty sure that the intersection of seafood with sweet corn is a meant-to-be thing. Clam, paprika and corn chowder is incredible, as is spicy corn-Manchego-lime salsa with garlicky sautéed whole prawns (do all of these things, please. You'll be happy). With that said, I'm not sure why I ever doubted this recipe – it is sweet and garlicky to the max, and it's exactly what you want with a side of warm bread.

Ingredients

2 shallots, peeled and finely chopped

1 tbsp vegetable oil

5 garlic cloves, peeled and minced

1 litre (34 fl oz/4 cups) low-sodium vegetable or chicken stock

2 tbsp fish sauce

200g (7½ oz) can sweetcorn, drained

220 g (8 oz) cooked, peeled and cleaned prawns

2 tbsp fresh coriander (cilantro), chopped

Preparation

In a large pan, fry the shallots in the oil over a medium heat until translucent, then add the garlic and cook for 1 minute. Add the stock and fish sauce and stir together. Leave to cook for 10 minutes while you prepare the corn.

Place the corn in a blender and pulse a few times, leaving some larger and smaller pieces. (Alternatively, place the corn in a bowl and use a hand-held blender to lightly mash the corn). Add to the pan with the prawns and heat through for 1 minute. Serve sprinkled with the fresh coriander.

UDON NOODLE & Mushroom Soup

[SERVES 3-4]

Given that it's taken me a while to start liking sushi I've become accustomed to ordering udon noodle soup at Japanese restaurants. It hardly ever disappoints with its thick, chopstick-friendly noodles and moreish broth. It's harder to get it right at home but once you've got the soup base down, the other ingredients are just a matter of preference (or what's left in the fridge). Mushrooms, peppers, leafy greens and squash are all good shouts and occasionally I'll crack in an egg for the last few moments of cooking. It's a lunchy comfort food that's incredibly filling and very useful for a fridge clear out.

Ingredients

2 tbsp soy sauce

3 tbsp brown miso paste

2 tbsp fish sauce

2 tsp peeled, grated ginger

2 spring onions (scallions), finely sliced

55 g (2 oz) mushrooms (enoki, button, portabello or shiitake), sliced

½ red (bell) pepper, de-seeded and finely sliced

300 g (10½ oz) fresh udon noodles or 200 g (7 oz) dry udon noodles

100 g (3½ oz) pak choi, kale or spinach

Preparation

In a large pan, combine the soy sauce, miso, fish sauce and ginger, then stir in 1½ litres (2½ pints/6 cups) water and bring to the boil over a medium heat.

Add the spring onions, mushrooms and pepper and cook for 5 minutes. Add the noodles, cooking them in the soup according to the directions on the packet. Meanwhile, roll up the pak choi (or other greens), slice into ribbons and add to the pan. Serve the soup as soon as the noodles are cooked.

CRISPY AUBERGINE
with Kale Pesto Fettuccine

[SERVES 4]

Next to charred aubergine (page 89), breaded and fried aubergine is my favourite thing.
Take those crispy, salty, creamy discs then bake them with tomato sauce and Parmesan and you have the
classic Aubergine Parmesan (or Eggplant Parmegian, as I grew up calling it). Instead of frying it, I've found
that baking the aubergine in the oven is simpler, healthier and less messy (no clearing up oil-filled pans!
Wooh!) It also gives you more free time to spend reading that magazine you've been wanting to
look at for months (or just making extra aubergine coins for snacks).

Ingredients

45 g (1½ oz/⅓ cup) plain (all-purpose) flour

1 egg

115 g (4 oz/1 cup) fine dry breadcrumbs

4 tbsp grated Parmesan, plus extra to serve

¼ tsp salt

½ tsp dried oregano

1 aubergine (eggplant), sliced into 1 cm (½ in)
   thick coins

2 tbsp olive oil

300 g (10½ oz) fettuccine
   (or spaghetti or tagliatelle)

1 quantity of Herby Kale Pesto (page 175)
   or 150 g (5 oz) store-bought pesto

Preparation

Preheat the oven to 200°C (400°F/Gas 6). Place the flour in a shallow bowl. In another shallow
bowl whisk the egg with 60 ml (2 fl oz/¼ cup) water. In a third shallow bowl, mix the breadcrumbs,
Parmesan, salt and oregano.

   Dip both sides of each aubergine coin first in the flour, then in the egg and finally in the
breadcrumbs. Lay them on a baking tray and drizzle or spray with olive oil. Bake for 10 minutes,
then flip them over and bake for a further 10–15 minutes until golden brown and crisp.

   Meanwhile, cook the pasta in a large pan filled with salted, boiling water according to the
instructions on the packet. Drain the pasta and stir in the pesto. Serve with the baked aubergine
and more Parmesan.

ROASTED VEGETABLE
+ Pesto Galette

[**MAKES 1 GALETTE (SERVES 4-6)**]

Can I tell you about how much I love pesto? If I can get it into a flavour-appropriate dish, I will. Stir it into soup, put it in panini, mix it with béchamel and pasta. Pesto-pasta and pesto-rice were childhood staples and I'm still not over them. Spreading it over a buttery, flaky pastry is even better, though. Especially when you're covering it with extra Parmesan and roasted vegetables, then eating it warm for dinner.

Ingredients

1 red (bell) pepper

10 cherry tomatoes, halved

½ quantity of Flaky Pastry (page 177), chilled for at least 30 minutes and up to 1 day, or a 250 g (9 oz) block of store-bought shortcrust pastry

5 tbsp pesto, store-bought or homemade such as Herby Kale Pesto (page 175)

75 g (2½ oz/⅓ cup) Parmesan, grated

1 courgette (zucchini), sliced into 5 mm (¼ in) thick coins

1 egg, beaten

Preparation

Preheat the oven to 200°C (400°F/Gas 6). Place the whole red pepper on a baking tray lined with foil and roast for 20 minutes. Use tongs to flip it over, then add the halved tomatoes to the tray, cut-side down, and roast for a further 20 minutes.

Remove from the oven and turn down the heat to 180°C (350°F/Gas 4). Poke a hole in the pepper to let out the steam then run it under cold water while you peel off the charred skin. Remove and discard the stalk and seeds from the pepper and slice the flesh into strips.

On a piece of baking parchment cut to the size of a large baking tray, roll out the pastry to a 30.5 cm (12 in) diameter circle. Spread the pesto over the pastry, leaving a 5 cm (2 in) border around the edge. Sprinkle with the Parmesan and cover with courgette coins, strips of roasted red pepper and the roasted tomatoes (still leaving that border).

Fold the uncovered edge of pastry up over the filling. Transfer the tart to the baking tray. Brush the pastry with beaten egg and bake for 30 minutes until golden brown. Serve with a green salad.

PORK RAGÙ WITH
Aubergine + Pappardelle

[SERVES 4]

There are certain ways of cooking things that simply transforms them. For me, charring aubergines is one of those ways. The aubergines take on an intense smoky flavour, making them taste as of you've spent ages attentively barbecuing them. In reality it takes minimal effort and you look like a superstar, fancy chef. If you have time to spare, the aubergine can be left to char in an oven. If you're in a rush then charring the aubergine over the flame of a gas stove is a quicker method.

Ingredients

2 aubergines (eggplants)

1 onion, peeled and finely chopped

2 tbsp olive oil

500 g (1 lb 2 oz) lean ground pork

400 g (14 oz) can chopped tomatoes

125 ml (4 fl oz/½ cup) red wine

1 tsp dried oregano

1 tsp fresh or dried rosemary

a handful of fresh basil

½ tsp salt

a large pinch of freshly ground black pepper

2 tbsp balsamic vinegar

1 tsp granulated sugar

300 g (10½ oz) pappardelle (or spaghetti
   or tagliatelle)

Parmesan shavings, to serve

Preparation

First, char the aubergines. In the oven: preheat the oven to 200°C (400°F/ Gas 6). Prick the aubergines all over with a fork then place on a foil-lined baking tray. Bake for 20 minutes, flip them over and bake for a further 20 minutes. On the stove top: prick the aubergines all over with a fork, place directly over the flame of a lit gas ring and cook for 15–20 minutes. Use tongs to turn the aubergines occasionally so all the skin is charred. (You may want to line the stovetop with foil for easy clean-up, as the aubergines tend to leak.)

Cut a slit down the centre of the aubergines and scoop out the flesh. Discard the skins and set the flesh aside.

In a large pan, sauté the onion in the oil over a medium heat until translucent. Add the pork and break it up with a wooden spoon into smaller pieces. Cook until the meat starts to brown then stir in the tomatoes, wine, herbs, salt, pepper, vinegar and sugar. Lower the heat and leave to simmer for 10 minutes.

Meanwhile cook the pasta in a large pot of salted water, boiling according to the instructions on the package. Drain the pasta, add it to the pan with the sauce and toss together.

Serve the pasta with the smoky aubergine mixed through, extra ragù from the pot, Parmesan shavings, extra basil and a little salt and pepper.

GRIDDLED CHICKEN *Salad*

[SERVES 2-4]

This recipe is perfect for when I'm in denial about summer ending but have to accept the arrival of autumn. I'm sitting around still making salads and pretending it's summer but getting an autumn food-fix from all those roasted sweet potatoes, the apple slices and pecans. A major note to self whenever I make this: in the time it takes to get roasted sweet potatoes from oven to plate I will have eaten at least twenty per cent of them. If you're the same as me, roast some extra sweet potato (snacks for the chef!) so you'll have enough left to actually feed other people.

Ingredients

4 sweet potatoes, peeled and cubed

a large pinch of dried chilli flakes

2 tbsp olive oil

2 boneless, skinless chicken breasts

a handful of fresh rosemary leaves, finely chopped

a large pinch each of salt and freshly ground black pepper

3 large handfuls of baby spinach

45 g (1½ oz/ ⅓ cup) pecans, roughly chopped

1 apple, cored and thinly sliced

Apple Cider-Honey Dressing

3 tbsp apple cider vinegar

1 tbsp honey

1 tbsp Dijon mustard

3 tbsp vegetable oil

a large pinch of salt

Preparation

Preheat the oven to 200°C (400°F/Gas 6). Place the sweet potatoes in a roasting tray and toss with the dried chilli flakes and half the olive oil. Roast for 30 minutes, flipping them over halfway through with a spatula.

Meanwhile, rub the chicken with the other tablespoon of oil, the rosemary and the salt and pepper. Place in a sandwich bag and seal. Bash the chicken with a rolling pin to flatten the breasts until they are about 2 cm (¾ in) thick.

Once you've flipped the potatoes, heat a griddle pan over a

medium heat and cook the chicken for 3–5 minutes on each side until golden brown and cooked all the way through. Cut into thick slices and layer with the spinach, pecans and sweet potato on a large plate.

Shake the dressing ingredients together in a lidded jar until emulsified. Toss the apple slices in some of the dressing then lay them on top of the salad. Drizzle the rest of the dressing over and serve warm or cold.

CHICKEN TACOS WITH
Peach BBQ Sauce

[SERVES 2-4]

Hello easy week-night meal! This is my absolute favourite meal to make when I want something insanely comforting to eat with very little active time and minimal prep. Usually, if I want to make chicken enchiladas or tacos, it involves either pre-frying the chicken or using more than one frying pan. Then there's the dry chicken problem — it gets over cooked pretty easily when cut into small chunks. Cooking the chicken in the sauce keeps it moist and flavoursome, plus you get that wonderful shredded chicken texture. Wrap it up with extra sauce, kale and sweetcorn and you have yourself an ideal dinner.

Ingredients

2 boneless, skinless chicken breasts

½ tsp salt

1 tsp ground cumin

2 tbsp apple cider vinegar

2 tsp hot smoked paprika

½ tsp ground cayenne

1 tsp ground cinnamon

1 shallot, peeled and finely chopped

1 tbsp vegetable oil

400 g (14 oz) can chopped tomatoes

2 peaches, stoned and roughly chopped

2 tbsp dark brown sugar

a large handful of kale, stems removed and
    leaves thinly sliced

½ green (bell) pepper, finely sliced

1 corn cob, kernels cut off

4 small soft tortillas

a handful of coriander (cilantro) leaves,
    to garnish

Preparation

In a small bowl, coat the chicken with the salt, cumin, vinegar, paprika, cayenne and cinnamon. Set aside for 10 minutes.

In a large pan, cook the shallot in the oil over a medium heat until translucent. Add the tomatoes, peaches and sugar, bring to a boil and then lower the heat to a simmer. Add the marinated chicken to the pan along with all of the marinade and leave to simmer for 30 minutes.

Place a steamer basket over a saucepan filled about halfway up with boiling water. Put the kale into the steamer basket, cover with the lid and cook for 10 minutes until tender.

Remove the chicken from the pan and shred the meat with two forks. Stir a few heaped tablespoons of the sauce into the shredded chicken and layer onto the tortillas with the steamed kale, sliced pepper, fresh corn kernels, coriander and more sauce.

SQUASH, PANCETTA
Cauliflower Risotto

[SERVES 3-4]

Risotto is a food to go to when all you want is carbs, carbs, carbs with a side of carbs. It's supremely creamy and starchy, plus you can put most vegetables in it (along with anything else you have in your fridge) and it'll be an assuredly brilliant dish. Asparagus, courgette (zucchini), spinach or mushrooms are all ace choices, but a certain combo will always be my favourite: roasted butternut squash and pancetta. The salty nuggets of pancetta are so good in risotto and make a power-couple pairing with the sweet, roasted squash. I also like to stir in some cauliflower (or pumpkin) purée for extra creaminess and a roasty, umami flavour.

Ingredients

½ head of cauliflower

1 butternut squash, peeled and seeds removed

4 tbsp olive oil

1 onion, peeled and finely chopped

4 garlic cloves, peeled and grated or minced

4 slices of bacon, cut into lardons

225 g (8 oz/1 cup) Arborio rice

1 litre (34 fl oz/4 cups) hot chicken or
    vegetable stock

250 ml (8½ fl oz/1 cup) dry white wine

½ tsp salt, plus more to taste

Parmesan shavings, to serve

Preparation

Preheat the oven to 200°C (400°F/Gas 6). Cut the cauliflower in half and place on a baking tray. Chop the butternut squash into 2.5 cm (1 in) cubes and place on the tray too. Drizzle with 2 tablespoons of olive oil and roast for 30 minutes until tender. Blitz the cooked cauliflower in a food processor or with a hand-held blender, or mash with a potato masher. Set the cauliflower purée and roasted squash chunks aside.

In a large pan, heat the remaining olive oil over a medium heat. Add the onion and cook until soft. Add the garlic and bacon and

cook until the bacon starts to crisp.

Pour the rice into the pan and cook for a few minutes, stirring, until it is slightly toasted. Add a quarter of the stock and cook, stirring, until it has been absorbed by the rice. Repeat this process with the rest of the stock and the wine.

Stir in the cauliflower purée and the salt and cook for a few more minutes to warm through. Serve with the roasted squash and Parmesan shavings.

SWEET & STICKY Pork

[SERVES 4]

Food markets are plentiful in London: if you're out in any pedestrianised shopping area you'll probably encounter one along the way. In central London there are stalls selling sweet roasted nuts, which (annoyingly) smell like vanilla toasted waffles. They attract my hungry, shopping-tired body from a mile away. If you go north or east, you'll most likely find stalls selling stir-fried noodles and sweet and sour chicken (the bright orange kind with chunks of pineapple). That ultra-sweet, sticky sauce doesn't seem oriental in any way but I've managed to come up with my own, spiced-up version for cooking with pork (or chicken). It's the treacly, dark brown sugar and star anise that enhance it, making a mouth-watering, shiny glaze with some tang and plenty of flavour.

Ingredients

400 g (14 oz) soba, udon, mung bean
   or rice noodles
1 tbsp vegetable oil
1 tbsp peeled, grated ginger
3 star anise
½ tsp chilli flakes
190 ml (6½ fl oz/¾ cup) sherry

125 ml (4 fl oz/½ cup) low-sodium vegetable
   stock or water
3 tbsp soy sauce
3 tbsp dark brown sugar
350 g (12 oz) pork loin, thinly sliced
fresh spinach leaves, to serve

Preparation

Cook the noodles according to the directions on the packet, then drain and set aside.

In a large frying pan, heat the oil over a high heat. Add the ginger, star anise and chilli flakes and mix in the sherry, stock, soy sauce and sugar. Add the pork and simmer for 5 minutes. Remove the pork from the pan, and continue to simmer the sauce for 2 minutes until it has reduced and is sticky.

Return the pork to the pan and stir to coat in the sauce. Serve on top of a handful of spinach leaves and the noodles, spooning over any sauce left in the pan (but leaving behind the star anise).

TUNA SALAD WITH Blackened Tomatoes

[SERVES 2-3]

Canned tuna is an ingredient that I feel that loads of people either resent or don't want
to admit they eat. It's a bit blah, normally just stirred up with some mayo and eaten in a sandwich. I'm giving
it some class here with blackened tomatoes (which sound mega fancy, but are actually very simple)
and cannellini beans. Using albacore tuna is best, as it has a better flavour than other tunas, and
the drizzle of lemon juice helps to cut through the fishy taste. The resulting salad is incredibly easy,
healthy and a tad sophisticated. I love eating it in the summer with hunks of sourdough
bread and thick balsamic vinegar.

Ingredients

200 g (7 oz) spinach
10 cherry tomatoes, halved
olive oil, for drizzling
salt and freshly ground black pepper

200g (7 oz) can albacore tuna, drained
400 g (14 oz) can cannellini beans, drained
    and rinsed
juice of ½ lemon

Preparation

Steam the spinach by cooking it with a small amount of water in a large, lidded pan for about
5 minutes, until just wilted.

Place the tomatoes cut-side down in a dry cast iron frying pan. Cook them over a medium heat
for 10 minutes — don't be tempted to touch them while they cook! Use a spatula to scrape them from
the pan. Drizzle a large salad plate with olive oil and arrange the spinach on top. Season with salt
and pepper. Flake the tuna over the spinach, sprinkle with the beans and tomatoes and squeeze the
lemon juice over the top.

TOMATO SOUP WITH Garlic + Pizzette

[SERVES 4]

* Vegan *

I have soup tricks up my sleeves: A roux base for a creamy texture and a splash of vinegar to pick up the flavours. I think I have the best of intentions when it comes to soup. It's comforting and mostly healthy and I do love it for those reasons but my main motivation is the bread you get with it for dipping. The little pizzas served with this soup are easy to make, garlic scented and adorned with a handful of rocket.

Ingredients

1 onion, peeled and finely chopped

1½ tbsp olive oil

2 tbsp plain (all-purpose) flour

250 ml (8½ fl oz/1 cup) almond (or other non-dairy) milk

½ teaspoon salt

½ teaspoon pepper

a handful of fresh basil leaves

3 tbsp balsamic vinegar

1 tbsp granulated sugar

2 x 400g (14 oz) cans tomatoes

500 ml (17 fl oz/2 cups) vegetable stock

The Pizzettes

3 garlic cloves, peeled and grated or minced

1½ tbsp olive oil

½ quantity of No-Knead Flatbread dough (page 179)

a few handfuls of rocket (arugula) leaves

flaky salt

Preparation

Note: Make the flatbread dough between 2 hours and 7 days before making the soup so it can rise. If you're making the dough more than 10 hours in advance, chill the dough until needed, then, just before making the soup, take the dough out of the fridge.

In a large saucepan, cook the onion with half the oil over a medium heat until translucent. Stir in the flour and cook for a minute. Gradually stir in the milk until incorporated. Stir in the rest of the soup ingredients and use a hand-held blender to blitz until smooth. Simmer for 20 minutes, stirring it occasionally.

Meanwhile, preheat a large ovenproof, non-stick frying pan

over a high heat. In a small bowl, stir together the garlic and olive oil. Preheat the grill to its highest setting.

Form the dough into 8 balls, dusted with flour. Flatten into 12.5 cm (5-in) diameter circles with a rolling pin. Place 2 circles of dough in the hot pan. Brush them with garlicky oil and top with some rocket leaves. Cook for 3 minutes (the underside of the dough will be browned) then place the pan under the grill for a further minute or so until puffed and golden. Remove the pizzettes from the pan and cook the remaining dough in the same way.

Serve warm pizzettes with the soup.

CARAMELISED ONION, Thyme + Bean Pot Pies

[SERVES 4]

When I learned how to caramelise onions I think it awoke some onion-hungry part of me that I never knew about before. I've since found that if you're in the kitchen caramelising onions don't doubt that you will attract pretty much anyone into that room. It's an intoxicating smell. I gave in and used them here bumping up the sweet, onion flavour with the addition of leeks too! Note: The recipe makes a perfectly satisfying soup if you make it without the pastry lid and simmer the mixture for an extra ten minutes.

Ingredients

2 onions, peeled and finely sliced

1 tbsp vegetable oil

1 leek, outer leaves removed, cleaned
    and finely sliced

a large pinch of salt

4 large carrots, thinly sliced into coins

3 tbsp plain (all-purpose) flour

750 ml (25 fl oz/3 cups) vegetable stock

125 ml (4 fl oz/½ cup) dry white wine

zest of 1 lemon

1 tsp fresh or dried thyme
    (plus some extra for garnishing)

400g (14 oz) can cannellini, butter or
    black-eyed beans, drained and rinsed

2 tbsp cream cheese (low-fat is fine)

salt and freshly ground black pepper, to taste

½ quantity of Flaky Pastry (page 177),
    chilled for at least 30 minutes

1 egg, beaten

Preparation

In a large, deep frying pan, dry-fry the onions, stirring over a medium heat until they start to brown. Add the oil, leek and salt, then continue to cook for about 20 minutes, until caramelised and golden.

Add the carrots and the flour over, then stir until everything is coated. Gradually stir in the vegetable stock and wine, then mix in the lemon zest, thyme, beans and cream cheese. Season to taste with salt and pepper and simmer for 5 minutes.

Divide the mixture between four 500 ml (16 oz) ramekins or

small pie dishes. Preheat the oven to 200°C (400°F/Gas 6).

Divide the pastry into 4 squares. On a lightly floured surface, roll out each square so it's a little bigger than a ramekin then trim the edges. Cover each filled ramekin with a square of pastry and pierce a cross into the top using a sharp knife to let out the steam as it cooks. Place the ramekins on a baking tray, brush the pastry with beaten egg and sprinkle with extra thyme leaves then bake for 35–45 minutes until completely golden.

[CHAPTER FOUR]

SWEET *Snacks*

CINNAMON PECAN + OATMEAL COOKIES

RAINBOW BISCOTTI CUBES

FROSTED RED VELVET CAKIES

BANANA BUCKWHEAT MUFFINS

MINI CHOCOLATE ONE CHUNK COOKIES (gluten-free)

WHOLEGRAIN DOUBLE CHOCOLATE MUFFIN MIX

BISCOTTI DI REGINA

SPANISH OLIVE OIL TORTAS

BEST CHOCOLATE CHIP COOKIES

MALTED PUMPKIN GINGERBREAD

RASPBERRY FRANGIPANE CAKE

CARAMELISED PIE CRUST S'MORES

I AM a messy baker; I can't help it. Seriously, I've tried being neat and it usually ends in disaster. It starts off OK: I'll bring out the ingredients one at a time for measuring, then put them back in the cupboard or drawer from which they came. I'll be thinking about how well this is going and praising the heck out of myself for being so organised and clean. Halfway through this neat baking process, something will always go wrong. I swear it's a legitimate curse. Thus, I give up the organised method and haul all the ingredients out again for round two. Once made, into the oven it goes with the timer set. By this stage I'll probably have lost the will to clean up the general mayhem that once was a kitchen, and so will leave the area entirely. This leads to another whole palaver involving listening out for the faint beeping of the oven timer, which I'll probably not hear until the second time it goes off and will subsequently have to power slide into the kitchen to save the batch of cookies from a smoky death. What is the point of me telling you this? Well, if someone like me, who prefers to bake in messy chaos, is capable of making these recipes, everyone is. I prefer simple baking methods that require minimal kitchen utensils (did I mention that I also hate washing dishes?) so if lack of fancy equipment is your main concern, don't worry. If you have a saucepan, bowl, spoon and whisk, chances are you too can make these recipes for your elevenses, 4 p.m. energy boost or low-key dessert.

CINNAMON PECAN & Oatmeal Cookies

[MAKES ABOUT 24 COOKIES]

My grammy passed her recipe for oatmeal cookies on to my mum, who wrote it down in her recipe book but says she could never make them 'the same way'. It turns out Mum hadn't written down the teaspoon of baking powder. She'd been making them for about twenty years without any leavening, ever since she moved from the US to London. After I eventually discovered the mistake and, given my inability to leave recipes alone, tweaked it, I ended up with these thin, crunchy cookies. They are quite different from the original ones but delicious all the same (and with the baking powder back in them!).

Ingredients

55g (2 oz/4 tbsp) unsalted butter

100 g (3½ oz/ 8 tbsp) coconut oil

100 g (3½ oz/½ cup) granulated sugar

150 g (5 oz/¾ cup) demerara (raw) sugar

1 egg

1 tbsp vanilla extract

1 tsp white wine/apple cider vinegar or lemon juice

½ tsp salt

¾ tsp baking powder

½ tsp bicarbonate of soda (baking soda)

1 tsp ground cinnamon

120 g (4 oz/1 cup) plain (all-purpose) flour

240 g (8½ oz/2½ cups) rolled oats

75 g (2½ oz/½ cup) chopped pecans

Preparation

Preheat the oven to 180°C (350°F/Gas 4) and line two baking trays with baking parchment.

Cream the butter, coconut oil and sugars together in a bowl using a wooden spoon or a hand-held electric beater. Mix in the egg and vanilla extract, then the vinegar and salt. Add the baking powder, bicarbonate of soda, cinnamon, flour and oats and stir until completely combined. Stir the pecans through.

Scoop 2 tablespoons of dough into a ball, place it on one of the lined baking trays and flatten it down with your hand. Repeat with the rest of the dough. Bake the cookies for 8–10 minutes, until golden brown around the edges. Leave the cookies on their trays for 1 minute, then transfer to a wire rack to cool completely.

. RAINBOW .
Biscotti Cubes

[MAKES 30 CUBES]

These cookies are way too cute. The chubby, rainbow-speckled cubes are loved by all and are the perfect size for stacking on the side of a coffee saucer, or piled up like little sugar cubes in a bowl. This biscotti dough isn't rock-hard when baked so you won't need to worry about any tooth-chipping mishaps. Lightly almond scented, these cookies are heavenly when enrobed in the white chocolate – perfect for a mid-morning snack with coffee.

Ingredients

125 g (4½ oz/1 cup) plain (all-purpose) flour

1 tsp baking powder

¼ tsp salt

65 g (2¼ oz/⅓ cup) granulated sugar

3 tbsp multicoloured sprinkles

1 egg, plus 1 egg white

1 tbsp amaretto liqueur or water

1 tsp almond extract

1 tbsp vegetable oil

100 g (3½ oz) white chocolate

Preparation

Preheat the oven to 180°C (350°F/Gas 4). In a large bowl, stir together the flour, baking powder, salt, sugar and sprinkles. Add the whole egg and egg white, amaretto or water, almond extract and oil. Stir together into a sticky dough.

Form the dough into a rectangle 10 x 12.5 cm (4 x 5 in) on a baking tray lined with baking parchment. Bake for 30 minutes until golden and firm.

Remove from the oven and while still on the tray, use a sharp knife to slice into roughly 2.5 cm (1 in) cubes. Spread the cubes out over the baking parchment and bake for a further 15 minutes. Leave to cool on the tray for 10 minutes.

Break the chocolate into pieces and place in a small heatproof bowl set over a pan of gently simmering water. Make sure the bottom of the bowl isn't actually touching the hot water. Use a wooden spoon to stir the chocolate until it is completely melted. It will take about 5 minutes. Dip a corner of each cube into the white chocolate then return it to the baking parchment and leave until the chocolate has set. Once set, transfer the biscotti to an airtight container (they will keep for up to a week).

FROSTED RED
Velvet Cakies

[MAKES 24 CAKIES]

Hello, what is this? Is it a little cake or a cookie? Neither. Well, it's both: it's a CAKIE!
You'll see people pick one up thinking they're cookies but then it's all, SURPRISE – it's actually
a cake pretending to be a cookie. It's the best of both worlds if you ask me, as we benefit from
a better cake-to-frosting ratio. Plus, when you'd normally only eat one cupcake, you can definitely
eat two cakies pretty casually. So that's twice as good really.

Ingredients

110g (3¾ oz/½ cup) unsalted butter

1 tsp vanilla extract

220 g (7¾ oz/1 cup) granulated sugar

2 eggs

4 tbsp sour cream or plain yoghurt

2 tbsp cocoa powder

1 tbsp red food colouring

250 g (9 oz/2 cups) plain (all-purpose) flour

1 tsp baking powder

Cream Cheese Frosting

75 g (2½ oz/6 tbsp) unsalted butter, softened

150 g (5 oz) cream cheese

1 tsp vanilla extract

150 g (5 oz/1½ cups) icing (confectioners')
   sugar

Preparation

Preheat the oven to 180°C (350°F/Gas 4). Line a baking tray with baking parchment.

Cream together the butter, vanilla extract and sugar in a medium bowl until fluffy. Stir in the eggs,
sour cream, cocoa powder and red food colouring until evenly combined. Stir in the flour and
baking powder.

Drop heaped tablespoons of the mixture onto the lined baking tray, spacing them about
2.5 cm (1 in) apart. Bake for 8 minutes, then transfer to a wire rack to cool.

Meanwhile, mix together all the frosting ingredients until smooth. Use a butter knife or palette
knife to swirl the frosting on top of the cakies. They can be stored in an airtight container for
3–4 days.

. BANANA .

Buckwheat Muffins

[MAKES 12 MUFFINS   ]

In my opinion, bananas are the best thing that can happen to quick breads. It makes perfect sense that once you throw fruit into a muffin batter it makes it more than OK to feel virtuous when eating one of those muffins. You're totally having fruit. There's fruit in this muffin and wholegrains and healthy fats. High-five me, and then have another. Have it with cream cheese, if you want. Second high-five for you.

Ingredients

3 large or 4 medium very ripe bananas, peeled

130 g (4½ oz/1 cup) buckwheat flour

65 g (2¼ oz/½ cup) wholemeal (whole-wheat) flour

2 tbsp olive oil

4 tbsp Almond Butter, store-bought or homemade (page 190)

150 g (5 oz/¾ cup) demerara (raw) sugar or coconut sugar, plus extra for sprinkling

2 tbsp ground flaxseed

125 ml (4 fl oz/½ cup) almond milk

1 tsp bicarbonate of soda (baking soda)

¼ tsp ground cinnamon

¼ tsp salt

12 walnut halves

Preparation

Preheat the oven to 180°C (350°F/Gas 4). Put all the ingredients, apart from the walnuts, in a food processor or blender and blitz until smooth. If you don't have a blender, mash the banana and then stir together with all the other ingredients, apart from the walnuts, in a large bowl.

Pour the batter into a 12-cup muffin tin lined with paper cases. Top each muffin with a walnut half (and a sprinkle of demerara sugar, if you want) and bake for 20–25 minutes.

. MINI CHOCOLATE .
One Chunk Cookies

[**MAKES 30 SMALL COOKIES**]

* Gluten-free *

These are the kind of cookies that you will want to eat while curled up, buried under a multitude of blankets with your best friends and a lame, wintery movie for company. So when it's getting cold and you're in the mood to cookie it up, wrap yourself in a blanket – cape style – and move your body into the kitchen so you can make these. Go, go! Get cookie-ing!

Note: Instead of using whole almonds and desiccated coconut you can use 275 g (10 oz/1¼ cup) natural Almond Butter (store-bought or homemade, see page 190) or peanut butter, and stir the mixture together in a bowl.

Ingredients

220 g (8 oz/1½ cups) almonds

55 g (2 oz/½ cup) desiccated or shredded coconut

4 tbsp ground flaxseed

1 egg

1 tbsp vanilla extract

200 g (7 oz/1 cup) brown sugar or coconut sugar

½ tsp salt

½ tsp bicarbonate of soda (baking soda)

¾ tsp baking powder

100 g (3½ oz/½ cup) dark (bittersweet) chocolate (minimum 60% cocoa solids), chopped

Preparation

Place the almonds and coconut in a food processor and blend until mealy. Continue to blend, scraping down the sides of the food processor with a rubber spatula as needed, until the mixture forms a paste.

Add the rest of the ingredients, apart from the chocolate, to the food processor and blend until well mixed. Stir in the pieces of chocolate.

Shape heaped teaspoons of the dough into balls and place them on a baking tray lined with baking parchment. Chill in the fridge for at least 1 hour or up to 7 days (the longer you leave them, the more flavour they will have – and it's worth it).

When you're ready to cook the cookies, preheat the oven to 180°C (350°F/Gas 4). Making sure the balls of dough are spaced 2.5 cm (1 in) apart on the lined baking tray, bake them for 5–7 minutes, until the edges are golden brown. Let them cool on the baking tray for a few minutes before transferring to a wire rack to cool completely. They will keep in an airtight container for up to 5 days.

WHOLEGRAIN DOUBLE
Chocolate Muffin Mix

[**ENOUGH FOR 16 MUFFINS /
4 BATCHES OF 4 MUFFINS**]

I love chocolate muffins, I really do. It takes a lot of will power to stick to ordering just a latte if I sense a chocolate muffin staring at me from the display counter in a café. It makes it easier when I know that there's a jar of chocolate muffin mix at home and all I have to do is stir in three ingredients to be rewarded with something way better than anything I'd ever buy. Muffins on demand? That's major.
Note: The oat flour in this recipe can be made by blending oats in a food processor until mealy.

Ingredients

The Muffin Mix

45 g (1½ oz/½ cup) oat flour (see note, above)
250 g (9 oz/2 cups) wholemeal (whole-wheat) flour
85 g (3 oz/1 cup) cocoa powder
2 tsp baking powder
2 tsp bicarbonate of soda (baking soda)
½ tsp salt
275 g (10 oz/1¼ cups) coconut sugar or granulated sugar
120 ml (4 fl oz/½ cup) vegetable oil or melted coconut oil

To Make 4 Muffins

200 g (7 oz/1¼ cups) muffin mix
1 egg
4 tbsp milk
15 g (½ oz) dark (bittersweet) chocolate
(minimum 60% cocoa solids), chopped

Preparation

To make the muffin mix: in a large bowl, stir together all the ingredients except for the oil, until well combined. Add the oil and use your hands to rub it into the dry ingredients. At this point you can store the mixture in an airtight container or jar. It will last for a month at room temperature or 3 months in the freezer.

To make the muffins: preheat the oven to 180°C (350°F/Gas 4). In a bowl, stir the muffin mix with the egg and milk until just combined. Divide between 4 cups of a muffin tin, lined with paper cases. Sprinkle the chopped chocolate over and bake for 20–25 minutes until a toothpick inserted into the centre of the muffins comes out clean. Transfer to a wire rack to cool (or eat them straight away!)

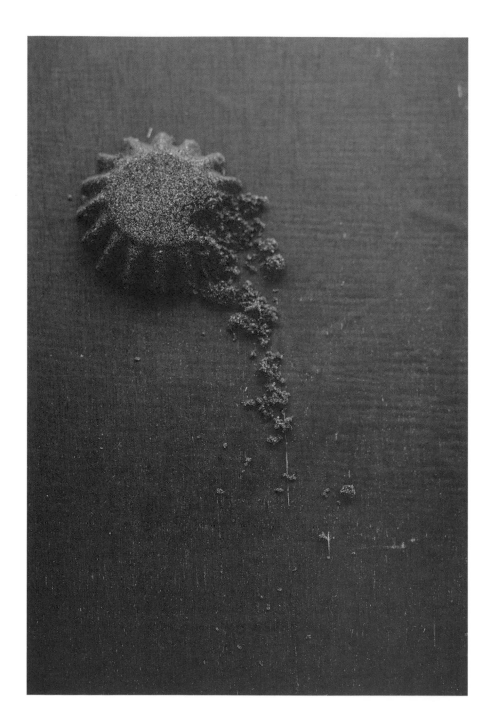

. BISCOTTI .
di Regina

[**MAKES ABOUT 30 COOKIES**   ]

I think I've found it: the key to pretending you're grown up is to bake things without chocolate in them. Even when you're spilling sesame seeds all over the counter, baking in an apron meant for a 12-year-old and dancing barefoot in the kitchen. We baked cookies with a fancy name! And they were totally easy. Do this, on the regular, and I guarantee that you'll have gained ten sophistication points by the time you're dunking these cookies into a mason jar of drip coffee.

Ingredients

240 g (8½ oz/2 cups) plain (all-purpose) flour

110 g (3¾ oz/½ cup) granulated sugar

1½ tsp baking powder

2 eggs

4 tbsp olive oil or vegetable oil

1 tsp vanilla extract or anise flavouring

a few handfuls of sesame seeds

Preparation

Preheat the oven to 180°C (350°F/Gas 4). In a large bowl, stir together the flour, sugar and baking powder. Add the eggs, oil and vanilla extract or anise and then mix until a dough is formed.

Divide the dough into 4 pieces and roll each piece into a 2.5 cm (1 in) thick snake. Cut into roughly 5 cm (2 in) lengths.

Tip the sesame seeds onto a plate and roll the lengths of dough in the seeds to coat them all over. Place on a baking tray lined with baking parchment and bake for 10 minutes until just browned on the bottom.

Transfer to a wire rack to cool. They will keep in an airtight container for up to 2 weeks.

· SPANISH OLIVE ·
Oil Tortas

[MAKES 8]

Visiting Borough Market is a basic 'must' if you're in London and interested in food. There's a stall there that sells imported Spanish goods, which is where I first saw these tortas being sold. I've since seen them in a few places, all sold the same way. They come individually wrapped in waxed paper and stacked up in packs of six. They're thin, flaky and utterly addictive but also waaay pricey. Goodbye new shoes, hello tortas. Luckily for us, it's easy to make them at home. I know some people seriously hate anise flavouring so you can leave it out if you insist, but I've found that most people love these with the anise.

Ingredients

215 g (7½ oz/1¾ cup) plain
  (all-purpose) flour

1½ tbsp demerara (raw) sugar

2 tbsp sesame seeds

½ tsp dried yeast

½ tsp salt

zest of 1 lemon

4 tbsp olive oil

½ tsp anise flavouring (optional)

90 g (3 oz/½ cup) large sugar crystals or
  crushed sugar cubes (white or unrefined)

Preparation

In a large bowl, combine the first 6 ingredients. Make a well in the centre and add the oil, anise (if using) and 80 ml (3 fl oz/⅓ cup) warm water. Use your hands to stir everything together and then knead into a ball.

Divide the mixture into 8 balls, place them on a baking tray lined with baking parchment and leave to rest at room temperature for 1 hour. Preheat the oven to 160°C (325°F/Gas 3).

On a lightly floured work surface, flatten each ball into a circle roughly 2 mm (⅛ in) thick. Transfer to a baking tray lined with fresh baking parchment. Using your fingertips, brush each one with a little water, then sprinkle with the sugar crystals. Bake for 10–15 minutes, rotating the tray 180 degrees halfway through. Let the tortas cool on a wire rack before serving.

BEST CHOCOLATE Chip Cookies

[MAKES 16 LARGE COOKIES]

Stop whatever you're planning on doing. New agenda: go and make this cookie dough now. Scoop it and put it into the fridge to rest. Resting the dough (for up to a week) ensures a more tender texture and a better flavour. You'll end up with the most kick-ass cookies you've ever tasted. Word to the wise – use chopped chocolate bars instead of chocolate chips, it's a stellar move – you'll get big melty puddles of chocolate in each cookie! I also like to infuse the butter with basil to add a slight 'jazz hands' quality.

Ingredients

4 tbsp fresh basil leaves (optional)

140 g (5 oz/10 tbsp) unsalted butter

1 tbsp vanilla extract

125 g (4½ oz/1 cup) plain (all-purpose) flour

85 g (3 oz/¾ cup) wholemeal (whole-wheat) flour

¾ tsp baking powder

¾ tsp bicarbonate of soda (baking soda)

110 g (3¾ oz/½ cup) granulated sugar

140 g (5 oz/½ cup, plus 3 tbsp) light brown sugar, packed

½ tsp flaky salt, plus more for sprinkling

1 egg

200 g (7 oz/1¼ cup) dark (bittersweet) chocolate (minimum 60% cocoa solids), roughly chopped

Preparation

Add the basil (if using) and butter to a small saucepan. If you're not using the basil, put the butter in the pan on its own. Heat over a medium-low heat until the butter foams up and smells nutty then stir in the vanilla extract.

Remove from the heat and cool for 10 minutes, then strain it through a sieve pushing through as much of the browned butter bits as possible – you're just trying to take out the basil. If you're not using the basil then you don't need to strain it.

Meanwhile, either use a stand mixer or a large bowl and a wooden spoon to combine the flours, baking powder, bicarbonate of soda, sugars and salt. Pour in the butter and mix until it looks like moist clumpy sand with no floury patches. Add the egg and mix in for a few seconds, then stir through the chopped chocolate until well distributed.

Using ¼ cup (60 ml/4 tbsp) cookie scoop or measuring cup, scoop up some of the dough and squash it into the scoop until it's just full. Turn out onto a baking parchment-lined baking tray. Repeat with the rest of the dough. If you don't have a cookie scoop or measuring cup, then divide the dough into 16 equal balls. Cover with cling film and refrigerate for between 1 hour and 7 days (the longer you wait, the better the texture and flavour!)

To bake: preheat the oven to 200°C (400°F/Gas 6) Making sure the cookies are spaced 7.5 cm (3-inches) apart, sprinkle them with salt. Bake for 8–12 minutes until browned with puffy, soft centres. Let them cool on the baking tray for 5 minutes then transfer to a wire rack. They will keep in an airtight container for up to 3 days.

MALTED PUMPKIN
Gingerbread

[**MAKES 1 MEDIUM LOAF CAKE**]

I'm going to have to use that word to describe this loaf: moist! It really is Caps Lock, exclamation mark, gone-in-a-day GOOD! The pumpkin purée keeps the gingerbread soft and sticky, more than any other gingerbread recipe I've ever used. The molasses make it dark enough to disguise the use of wholemeal flour from picky eaters. And the taste is just like winter and the definition of the word 'cosy' in the form of a quick bread.

Ingredients

85 g (3 oz/ 6 tbsp) unsalted butter

65 g (2¼ oz/¼ cup, plus 1 tbsp) dark brown sugar

100 g (3½ oz/¼ cup) golden syrup, agave syrup or maple syrup

3 tbsp unsulfured molasses

⅛ tsp ground cloves

½ tsp ground cinnamon

1 tsp ground ginger

¾ tsp bicarbonate of soda (baking soda)

1 egg

125 ml (4½ oz/½ cup) pumpkin purée (see below) or apple sauce

1½ tbsp malted milk powder

130 g (4½ oz/1 cup, plus 1 tbsp) wholemeal (whole-wheat) flour

a handful of candied ginger, roughly chopped

Preparation

Note: To make pumpkin purée, halve a small pumpkin or butternut squash and remove the seeds. Preheat the oven to 200°C (400°F/Gas 6) and roast the pumpkin halves on a baking tray for 45 minutes. Scoop out the soft flesh and blitz until smooth. You can freeze it for up to 3 months.

Preheat the oven to 180°C (350°F/Gas 4). Grease a 21 cm (8½ in) loaf tin with a little sunflower oil and then line it with baking parchment.

In a large saucepan over a medium heat, gently stir the butter, sugar, syrup and molasses together until the butter is melted.

Remove from the heat and stir in the cloves, cinnamon, ginger and bicarbonate of soda. Beat in the egg and pumpkin purée, then the malted milk powder, and finally stir in the flour. Pour the batter into the prepared tin and bake for 10 minutes. Quickly pull the tin out of the oven and sprinkle the candied ginger down the centre, then return it to the oven to continue cooking for a further 35 minutes. Let the loaf cool for 10 minutes in the tin before turning it out onto a wire rack to cool completely.

. RASPBERRY .
Frangipane Cake

[**SERVES 12-16**]

My mum has an uncanny skill for ordering the best food at cafés and restaurants. Luckily, she's also generous with sharing! We'll usually order two things and split them between us. One time she ordered a streusel-topped muffin (I had gone for a bittersweet chocolate croissant) and I swear that it had gone even before our coffees had arrived. You see, it was no ordinary muffin. *Cue inspirational music! It was to muffins what a fancy latte is to instant coffee. Embedded with an almond paste mixture and dotted with raspberries. Endlessly buttery and moreish. This recipe is my homage to that muffin, but bigged-up, cake style.

Ingredients

250 g (9 oz/2 cups) plain (all-purpose) flour

165 g (5⅔ oz/¾ cup) granulated sugar

2 tsp baking powder

¼ tsp bicarbonate of soda (baking soda)

¼ tsp salt

150 g (5 oz/⅔ cup) unsalted butter, cubed

80 ml (2¾ fl oz/⅓ cup) plain yoghurt

2 eggs

1 tsp almond extract

1 quantity of Frangipane (page 183)

110 g (3¾ oz/1 cup) raspberries, fresh or frozen

Preparation

In a large bowl, combine the flour, sugar, baking powder, bicarbonate of soda and salt. Add the butter cubes and rub them in with your fingertips until no large chunks of butter remain. Remove 100g (3½ oz) of this crumbly mixture and set aside for the topping.

Pour the yoghurt, eggs and almond extract into the remaining mixture and stir until just combined. Pour into a greased and floured, deep 20 cm (8 in) cake tin. Preheat the oven to 180°C (350°F/ Gas 4).

Dollop the frangipane over the surface of the batter and swirl it through lightly with a knife. Cover with the raspberries and then with the reserved crumbly mixture.

Bake for 45–50 minutes, covering with foil after 30 minutes, if needed, to prevent the streusel from burning. Leave to cool on a wire rack for at least 20 minutes before serving.

CARAMELISED
Pie Crust S'mores

[MAKES 8]

So you've just made a pie. A beautiful, delicious pie. Now there are all these scrappy pieces of unbaked pastry sitting in a ball on your counter. I always feel sad throwing away pastry scraps (I made that with my HANDS, man). It's such a shame to waste something so delicious, but I've found the perfect solution: roll out any pastry scraps using a mixture of flour and sugar to dust your work surface, and bake them with a little cinnamon-sugar sprinkled on top. The sugar embedded in the pastry caramelises and crisps so you end up with something like an American graham cracker. And if you sandwich them with super-dark chocolate, a toasted marshmallow and a pinch of flaky salt, they make the perfect s'mores.

Ingredients

plain (all-purpose) flour, for rolling
demerara (raw) sugar, for rolling
any quantity of un-baked pastry
    (flaky pastry is especially good)
2 tbsp ground cinnamon

4 tbsp granulated sugar
dark (bittersweet) chocolate chips or large,
    thin squares (minimum 60% cocoa solids)
flaky salt, for sprinkling
large marshmallows, halved lengthways

Preparation

Preheat the oven to 180°C (350°F/Gas 4). Dust your work surface with a mixture of equal parts flour and demerara sugar. Sprinkle the pastry with a little of the flour and demerara sugar, too. Roll out the pastry to a thickness of about 3 mm (⅛ in).

In a small bowl, stir together the cinnamon and granulated sugar. Cover the surface of the dough with the cinnamon-sugar (there may be some left over, depending on how much pastry you have). Use your rolling pin to gently push the cinnamon-sugar into the surface of the pastry.

Cut into 5 cm (2 in) squares and bake on a baking tray lined with baking parchment for 10–15 minutes until golden brown.

To make s'mores, flip the squares over, and transfer half of them to a wire rack. Sprinkle these squares with chocolate chips or top with a square of chocolate and a little flaky salt. Set aside, letting the chocolate melt. Preheat the oven to 200°C (400°F/Gas 6) or heat the grill to its highest setting.

While the oven or grill is heating, top each square still on the baking tray with a halved marshmallow, cut-side down. Bake or grill until golden brown — watch them closely so they don't burn. Sandwich a marshmallow-topped and chocolate-topped square together and eat immediately.

[CHAPTER FIVE]

. DESSERTS .

ROASTED BLUEBERRY FROZEN YOGHURT

BOOZY MOCHA COCONUT LAYER CAKE

CHOCOLATE POTS DE CRÈME

CHOCOLATE CHIP AMARETTO TORTE

SWEDISH CHOCOLATE CAKE

CRUSTLESS PLUM + ALMOND TART

GRILLED FRUIT WITH SALTED BROWN SUGAR

CAPPUCCINO CAKE

DUTCH APPLE CAKE

MUM'S TIRAMISU

COCONUT MACAROON BROWNIES

STICKY BANOFFEE CAKE WITH SALTED CARAMEL

BROWNED BUTTER CRUMBLE BLUE-BARB PIE

PEAR, FRANGIPANE + CARAMEL TARTLETS

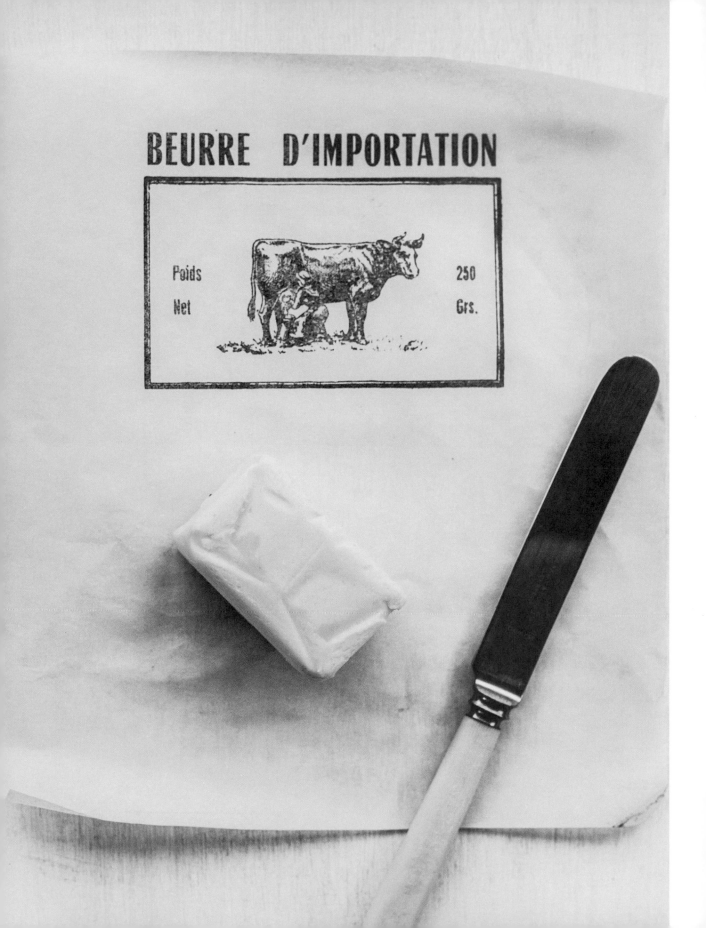

I'VE BECOME the notorious dessert creator for family occasions and birthdays. It's always an issue trying to come up with things to make when I'm feeding dessert to my food-loving, extended family multiple times a year, because I run out of ideas. Thankfully, there's a failsafe collection of bakes that have either been made up by me or are go-to recipes that have been written down in the family cookbook over the years. I think you can tell that you've found a really good recipe if you fall back on it multiple times, and these recipes are just that. Some will take longer to make than others (baking and frosting a three-layer cake isn't exactly a quick fix!) but I've kept the decoration and preparation simple. I'm not crazy for piping buttercream or rolling out fondant because the food is always gone in such a short space of time! I'd much rather leave it to be what it is, naturally pretty, because it's so much more satisfying that way. As someone who loves styling and photographing food, I naturally tend to put more time than is warranted into presentation, though, so if the food comes out a little messy, call it rustic or artisanal and you'll be good to go! But, P.S., if you're giving someone cake, chances are they won't care about how it looks. Take it from someone who has brought frosted cakes into school, on her bike and on the underground during rush-hour, in cake tins that only fit into a bag sideways. 'Yeah, that messed up frosting on the side is rustic. It's rustic, shhhh.'

ROASTED BLUEBERRY
Frozen Yoghurt

[SERVES 4-8]

Much like how I complain in the winter that 'It's so freezing outside, I can't even feel my
face any more', there are those (rare) summer days when I find it 'Too hot to even look at the stove.'
Therefore, come late July. it's fro-yo time. Unlike ice cream, frozen yoghurt doesn't require
constant stirring of a liquid base over a hot stove. However, you do have to turn the oven on to roast the
blueberries for this recipe, so just throw those berries in there and get the heck out of the kitchen
for the next ten minutes. When opening the oven door just think of the cold, creamy fro-yo as your reward
for braving the heat — you just earned an extra scoop.

Ingredients

125 g (4½ oz/1 cup) blueberries

3 tbsp demerara (raw) sugar

625 ml (21 fl oz/2½ cups) Greek yoghurt
(it's best not to use low-fat stuff here)

4 tbsp honey or agave syrup

3 tbsp lemon juice

Preparation

Preheat the oven to 200°C (400°F/Gas 6). Scatter the blueberries over a baking tray with a deep
edge and sprinkle with the sugar. Roast for 10 minutes, until most of the blueberries have burst, then
leave to cool on the tray.

In a jug, stir together the yoghurt, honey, cooled blueberries and lemon juice. If you want, you
can use a hand-held blender to make the mixture smooth. Churn in an ice cream maker according
to the manufacturer's directions. Serve immediately or freeze for up to 3 weeks.

· BOOZY MOCHA ·
Coconut Layer Cake

[SERVES 8-12]

This is pretty much a huge lamington – minus the jam, plus some coffee and coffee liqueur. So ... it's not really a lamington in the end but those are some good changes right!? Even people who insist that they don't like coconut (a.k.a. my dad) will devour this cake.

Ingredients

110g (3¾ oz/½ cup) unsalted butter

220 g (7¾ oz/1 cup) granulated sugar

3 eggs

1 tsp vanilla extract

½ tsp salt

2 tsp baking powder

4 tbsp desiccated or shredded coconut, plus
   a little extra for decoration

290 g (10 oz/2⅓ cups) plain
   (all-purpose) flour

310 ml (10 fl oz/1¼ cups) milk

1 quantity of Chocolate Ganache (page 184)
   (let it cool in the fridge for at least 30 minutes)

Coffee Syrup

3½ tbsp granulated sugar

1 tbsp instant coffee granules

4 tbsp coffee liqueur or water

Preparation

Preheat the oven to 180°C (350°F/ Gas 4). Line, grease and flour three 20 cm (8-inch) cake pans as shown on pages 194–5.

In a large bowl, cream together the butter and sugar until pale and fluffy. Stir in the eggs, one at a time, then mix in the vanilla extract, salt, baking powder and coconut. Mix in half the flour, then half the milk, then the remaining flour and then the milk.

Divide the mixture between the prepared tins and bake for 30–35 minutes until a toothpick inserted into the middle comes out clean. Cool the cakes in their tins for 10 minutes, then turn out onto a wire rack. Remove the parchment paper and turn the cakes right side up again. Leave to cool completely then level any domed cakes with a serrated knife.

Make the coffee syrup by heating the sugar and instant coffee with 125 ml (4 fl oz/½ cup) boiling water in a small saucepan for

5 minutes, stirring until the sugar has dissolved. Remove from the heat and stir in the coffee liqueur (or additional water).

To assemble: place 1 cooled cake (cut side down, if levelled) on a large platter. Use a pastry brush or teaspoon to soak the entire top of the cake with the syrup. Place about 2 heaped tablespoons of ganache on top and use a blunt knife to spread it over the surface of the cake, stopping just shy of the edge. Top with the second cake layer (cut side down) and press down slightly. As before, cover with coffee syrup and ganache then top with the third cake (cut side down). Spoon the remaining ganache on top of the cake, smoothing it out cake's surface. Bring it right to the edge and halfway down the side of the top layer. Sprinkle with some coconut. The cake will keep in an airtight container for up to a week.

CHOCOLATE POTS
de Crème

[SERVES 6]

I think I'm going to have you warn you that, a) halfway through eating one of these you may think you need to stop eating it and, b) you won't stop eating it. These little pots are total people-pleasers (particularly if there are chocoholics around) and I'm going to give you a sneaky tip: even though they sound fancy (i.e. make it seem like you've gone all out), they're actually fifty times easier to make than chocolate mousse. Simply blend and chill. They're cool, you're cool. It's all cool.

Ingredients

170 g (6 oz) dark (bittersweet) chocolate
   (minimum 60% cocoa solids)
1 tsp vanilla extract
a pinch of salt

285 ml (10 fl oz/1 cup plus 2 tbsp) single, light
   or whipping cream
1 egg
crumbled Amaretti biscuits, to serve (optional)*

Preparation

Place the chocolate in a blender with the vanilla extract and salt.

In a small saucepan heat the cream over medium-low heat until just steaming. Pour the hot cream into the blender and blitz until smooth.

Add the egg and blitz again. Divide the mixture between 6 ramekins, small bowls or glasses and chill for at least 3 hours until set. For added texture, serve with crumbled Amaretti biscuits on top.

* Amaretti biscuits aren't gluten free but the Pots de Crème themselves are.

CHOCOLATE CHIP Amaretto Torte

[MAKES 8–12]

So, apparently, coming from a foodie family instils fear into other people when they are tasked with feeding you. IS THIS PASTA OK? What about the SALAD? Let me watch your face while you eat, Izy. Mate, you're giving me food! Food you've cooked! Hey, I like that! I'm not a food critic and I ain't mean. Let's just chill out. I've brought dessert, it's a chocolate chip torte that's so classy/un-classy that we'll all forget about how stressful this was and focus on trying not to inhale and subsequently choke on the icing sugar dusted on top. Good times, good times.

Ingredients

4 eggs

¼ tsp salt

110 g (3¾ oz/½ cup) granulated sugar

110 g (3¾ oz/½ cup) unsalted butter

75 g (2½ oz/½ cup) plain (all-purpose) flour

45 g (1½ oz/½ cup) ground almonds

1 tsp baking powder

110 g (3¾ oz/½ cup) crushed Amaretti biscuits

2 tbsp amaretto liqueur

75 g (2½ oz/½ cup) plain (bittersweet) chocolate chips (minimum 60% cocoa solids)

1 tbsp icing (confectioners') sugar

Preparation

Preheat the oven to 180°C (350°F/Gas 4). Line, grease and flour a 20 cm (8 in) tart or cake tin, as shown on pages 194–5.

Separate the eggs into 2 large bowls. Whisk the egg whites with the salt until soft peaks form, then continue to whisk while gradually adding half the granulated sugar until you get firm peaks.

Add the butter and remaining sugar to the bowl with the egg yolks and cream together until fluffy. Stir in the flour, ground almonds, baking powder, crushed Amaretti biscuits and the amaretto liqueur.

Stir one-quarter of the whisked egg whites into the almond mixture to loosen it. Add the rest of the egg whites and gently fold in using a rubber spatula.

Pour the mixture into the prepared tin and sprinkle with chocolate chips. Bake for 25 minutes and let cool completely in the tin before turning out onto a plate. Set a wire rack on top and then flip the whole thing over so that the torte is the right way up again. Dust with icing sugar and serve.

. SWEDISH .
Chocolate Cake

[MAKES 8-9]

I'm throwing a bold claim in here: this is the best chocolate cake you'll ever make. It's wonderfully quick since it's all melted together in one pot and poured straight into the cake tin. Bake it carefully — keep it gooey! I'll cry if you over-bake it, OK? It requires no frosting, only a dusting of icing sugar but looks just as impressive as a four-layer cake with buttercream roses … It'll be gone in a day, though, so don't make any plans for it any longer than five hours post-bake. No worries though, you can just make another one because it was so darn easy the first time!

Ingredients

135 g (4¾ oz/10 tbsp) salted butter

55 g (2 oz/½ cup) cocoa powder

350 g (12 oz/1¾ cups) granulated sugar

1 tsp vanilla extract

110 g (3¾ oz/1 cup, minus 2 tbsp) plain
(all-purpose) flour

3 eggs

2 tbsp icing sugar (confectioners') sugar,
for dusting

Preparation

Preheat the oven to 180°C (350°F/Gas 4). Line, grease and flour a deep 18 cm (7 in) cake tin, as shown on pages 194–5.

Melt the butter in a medium saucepan. Remove from the heat and stir in the rest of the ingredients. Pour the mixture into the prepared cake tin and bake for 20–30 minutes — it should be set around the edges but still gooey in the middle.

Let the cake cool in its tin for about 20 minutes, then run a blunt knife around the inside edge of the tin to loosen it. Turn out onto a wire rack, dust with icing sugar and serve warm.

CRUSTLESS PLUM + Almond Tart

[SERVES 9-12]

When the summer starts winding down and fall fruits are coming into season, I love making plum tarts with puff pastry and frangipane. Most of the time I am definitely happy to eat pastry, but with those tarts I always wish for more filling (P.S. I am a major frangipane fiend). This is my solution: a plum tart without the pastry. It is a bulked-up frangipane mixture studded with ruby red plums and baked until puffed with a texture somewhere between a dense cake, a blondie and an almond macaroon. It's equally good with other fruits, like blueberries or sliced apple, OR you can replace the almond extract with vanilla and sprinkle on some chocolate chips instead of the fruit to make gluten-free blondies!

Note: The oat flour in this recipe can be made by blending oats in a food processor until mealy.

Ingredients

90 g (3 oz/6 tbsp) unsalted butter
140 g (5 oz/⅔ cup) granulated sugar
4 tbsp maple, agave or golden syrup
1 egg
1 tsp almond extract
¼ tsp salt
½ tsp baking powder

95g (3¼ oz/1 cup) ground almonds
70 g (2½ oz/¾ cup) oat flour
   (see note, above)
4 plums, quartered, de-stoned and each
   quarter cut into thirds
1 tbsp icing sugar (confectioners') sugar

Preparation

Preheat the oven to 180°C (350°F/Gas 4). Grease and line a 25 x 18 cm (7 x 10 in) or a 20 cm (8 in) square tin with baking parchment.

Melt the butter in a medium saucepan. Remove from the heat and stir in the sugar and syrup. Quickly beat in the egg, almond extract, salt and baking powder. Stir in the ground almonds and oat flour until you have a smooth batter.

Tip the batter into the prepared tin and spread it out evenly. Decorate the top with the slices of plum and bake for 25–30 minutes until golden brown. Dust with the icing sugar and leave to cool a little on a wire rack before slicing and serving. The tart can be served warm or at room temperature on its own or with crème fraîche or Greek yoghurt.

GRILLED FRUIT WITH
Salted Brown Sugar

[MAKES 6]

As soon as peaches are finally cheap in the markets, no one can stop me eating as many of them as humanly possible. I will eat them for breakfast, post-cycle snack, dessert … and also just any time I see a peach. When I visited a market in Paris last year the people at the stalls were offering slices of peach just for looking at the fruit. I left the market having eaten a lot of free peach slices, and with a paper bag full of them. Most of the time you don't get to 'try before you buy' and can end up with unripe or just utterly flavourless fruit. This can be helped by grilling the peaches, which makes them tender and juicy. The dark brown sugar, vanilla and cinnamon in this recipe caramelise on the fruit and their flavours mingle together in the baking tray. Top with some tangy crème fraîche or vanilla ice cream and you'll have the epitome of summer in a dessert.

Ingredients

3 peaches

3 bananas

4½ tbsp dark brown sugar

1 tsp vanilla extract

¼ tsp flaky salt

¼ tsp ground cinnamon

3 tbsp demerara (raw) sugar

to serve: pecans, flaked coconut and crème
fraîche or vanilla ice cream

Preparation

Preheat the oven to 200°C (400°F/Gas 6). Halve the peaches and remove the stones. Halve the bananas lengthways (still in their skins). Place the halved fruit cut-side up on a large baking tray with a deep edge.

In a small bowl, stir together the brown sugar, vanilla extract, salt and cinnamon. Divide the mixture between the fruits, spreading it over the cut surfaces, then cook in the oven for 20 minutes. Remove from the oven and use a spoon to baste the fruit with any juice that has pooled in the tray. Sprinkle the fruit with the demerara sugar. Heat the grill to its highest setting.

Grill the fruit for 2–5 minutes, watching closely until the sugar is caramelised. Serve with pecans, flaked coconut and crème fraîche or ice cream.

CAPPUCCINO *Cake*

[**SERVES 9–12**]

I face a constant dilemma when it comes to talking about coffee cake. Are you telling me about a coffee-flavoured cake, or the streusel-topped cake, popular in America, that is eaten with a cup of coffee? After visiting my grammy in Boston, my mum brought back a recipe from one of her friends. It was a recipe for Secret Sour Cream Coffeecake. I asked mum about the lack of coffee and she laughed at me but eventually explained the difference. That's why I've called this Cappuccino Cake, so you won't flick to the page expecting a fruity brunch cake. Instead you'll know I'm talking pure coffee flavour, and this cake delivers. The sponge and buttercream are unashamedly infused with it, then it's topped with coffee-whipped cream and dusted with cocoa powder, so it even looks vaguely cappuccino-like!

Ingredients

250 g (9 oz/2¼ cups) plain (all-purpose) flour
3 tsp baking powder
50 g (2 oz/½ cup) ground almonds
220 g (7¾ oz/1 cup) granulated sugar
½ tsp salt
110 g (3¼ oz/½ cup) unsalted butter
3 tbsp instant coffee granules
80 ml (3 fl oz/⅓ cup) milk
3 eggs

Frosting and Filling

2 tbsp instant coffee granules
125 ml (4 fl oz/½ cup) whipping cream
360 g (12 oz/3 cups) icing (confectioners') sugar, plus 2 tbsp
110 g (3¾ oz/½ cup) unsalted butter, cut into small cubes
2 tbsp cocoa powder

Preparation

Preheat the oven to 180°C (350°F/Gas 4). Line, grease and flour three 20 cm (8 in) cake tins, as shown on pages 194–5.

In a large bowl, mix together the flour, baking powder, ground almonds, sugar and salt. Using your fingers, rub the butter into the dry ingredients until no large chunks of butter remain.

Dissolve the coffee in 80 ml (3 fl oz/⅓ cup) hot water and pour into the flour mixture, along with the milk and eggs. Mix together using a wooden spoon or a hand-held electric beater.

Divide the batter between the lined cake tins and bake for

20–25 minutes until the cake springs back when poked with a finger. Let the cakes cool in their tins for 10 minutes, then turn out onto a wire rack. Remove the baking parchment and turn the cakes right-side up. Leave to cool completely before using a serrated knife to level any domed cakes.

To make the filling and frosting, combine 2 tablespoons of boiling water and the instant coffee in a small bowl. In a large bowl, whisk the cream until it just starts to thicken. Add the 2 tablespoons of icing sugar and 1 tablespoon of the

dissolved coffee. Continue to whisk until it forms soft peaks (if it starts to look grainy, immediately add 2 tablespoons of extra whipping cream and gently stir it in). Chill in the fridge while you make the buttercream.

Make the coffee buttercream by creaming the butter, remaining dissolved coffee and the icing sugar together in a separate bowl until smooth. It should be the consistency of cream cheese so add a splash of milk if it seems too thick.

To assemble, place 1 cooled cake (cut-side down, if levelled) on a cake stand or large platter. Place one-third of the buttercream on top of the cake and use a spoon or butter knife to spread it over the surface of the cake, stopping just shy of the edge. Top with a second cake (again, cut-side down) and press down lightly so that the buttercream is pushed to the edge. As before, cover with buttercream and then top with the third cake (cut-side down).

Use the remaining buttercream to very thinly frost the side of the cake (this is known as a crumb coating). Use the coffee-whipped cream to frost the top of the cake. To create the effect shown in the photograph, use a palette knife to create C-shapes in the whipped cream, starting at the top of the cake and moving towards the centre. Do this all along the edge of the cake until you've covered the entire surface, then dust with cocoa powder. The cake will keep in the fridge for a couple of days; bring it to room temperature before serving.

. DUTCH .
Apple Cake

[SERVES 8-9]

Do I have any idea why this is known as Dutch Apple Cake? Nope. There are many randomly
named recipes written down in our family recipe book, this being one. The 'Blanc Mange' (which is actually
a recipe for Swiss-roll cake) and 'Sinking Red Devils Food Cake' (which neither sinks nor is red)
being others. But I do know that all of these recipes are foolproof, simple and comforting. This apple cake is
unlike any I've ever come across. The apples are thinly sliced and pushed into the top of the cake in a
star-like pattern, with only the thin outer edge of the fruit showing. When baked, the exposed part of the
apple dries, becoming slightly chewy, while the batter-covered portion is soft and sweet.

Ingredients

110 g (3¼ oz/½ cup) unsalted butter

220 g (7¾ oz/1 cup) granulated sugar

¼ tsp grated nutmeg

2 eggs

2½ tsp baking powder

½ tsp salt

250 g (9 oz/2 cups) plain (all-purpose) flour

190 ml (6½ fl oz/¾ cup) milk

2 eating apples, peeled, cored and halved

2 tbsp demerara (raw) sugar

Preparation

Line, grease and flour a deep 20 cm (8 in) cake tin, as shown on pages 194–5. Preheat the oven to
180°C (350°F/Gas 4).

In a large bowl, cream together the butter, sugar and nutmeg. Beat in the eggs, one at a time, and
add the baking powder and salt. Stir in half of the flour, then half of the milk, then the rest of the
flour and the rest of the milk. Pour the batter into the prepared pan.

Thinly slice the apple halves and arrange them in the cake batter in a star shape, pushing the
slices in so that only the thin outside edge shows on top. Make sure you really pack the apple slices
in, as they will shrink during baking. Sprinkle with the demerara sugar and bake for 35–40 minutes
until a toothpick inserted into the centre of the cake comes out clean.

. MUM'S .
Tiramisu

[**SERVES 8-10**]

There was a brief period when I didn't have access to an oven. It was about three months of
no baking but it felt like an eternity, no joke. I ended up resorting to awkwardly inviting myself round to my
best friend's house to use their oven, and creating no-bake desserts at home. Tiramisu was obviously one
of those desserts, given that it is one of my favourite things to eat. It's a total cliché to say this but
my mum's tiramisu recipe is definitely the best. Nobody denies it and everyone wants the recipe. I think the
secret lies in the tonne of booze that is generously laced into both the creamy filling and
spongy ladyfingers. Oh, oh, and the thick layer of cocoa powder dusted on top. I am telling you, don't
be stingy with the cocoa powder; dust it all on. It'll sink in and make a nice bitter layer to cut through the
sweetness and strength of the rest of the dessert.

Ingredients

4 egg yolks

220g (7¾ oz/) mascarpone

55 g (2 o/8 tbsp) plain yoghurt

85 g (2¾ oz/½ cup) icing (confectioners') sugar

100 ml (3½ fl oz/½ cup) dry white wine

185 ml (6¼ fl oz/¾ cup) Marsala wine

250 ml (9 oz/1 cup) strong freshly brewed coffee

20–30 ladyfinger (savoiardi) biscuits

3–4 tbsp cocoa powder

Preparation

To make the cream, whisk together the egg yolks, mascarpone, yoghurt, sugar, the white wine and
100 ml (3½ fl oz/½ cup) of the Marsala in a large jug.

In a shallow bowl or dish, stir together the coffee and remaining Marsala. Dip the ladyfingers
into this mixture briefly and then arrange them in a single layer in a large dish, 21 x 28 cm (8 x 11 in)
or 23 cm (9 in) square, or small, individual glasses (you may have to break up the biscuits to get them
to fit). Pour on some of the cream mixture until the biscuits are just covered. Top with another layer
of coffee-soaked biscuits and then more cream. Repeat these layers until all the cream has been
used up, finishing with a layer of cream.

Dust very generously with the cocoa powder and place in the fridge to chill for at least 24 hours
before serving.

. COCONUT .
Macaroon Brownies

[**SERVES 9-16**]

During the Christmas holidays there seem to be chocolate selection boxes everywhere –
purple and red tins are all over the place. You can't turn up to school during December without being
offered some kind of confectionery. And when a new tin is opened, a stampede of people run
towards the chocolate-bringer. Their aim? To make sure they're not left with the fruit-goo or coconut-filled
chocolates. Luckily, I love the coconut chocolates so I'm glad to be, um, 'burdened' with them. These brownies
take inspiration from the flavours of those chocolates, translating them into fudgy brownie form.

Ingredients

110 g (3¾ oz/½ cup) unsalted butter
100 g (3½ oz) dark (bittersweet) chocolate
   (minimum 60% cocoa solids)
220 g (7¾ oz/1 cup) granulated sugar
2 tsp vanilla extract

2 eggs, plus 1 egg white
60 g (2 oz/½ cup) plain (all-purpose) flour
¼ tsp salt
240 g (8½ oz/1½ cups) desiccated or
   shredded coconut

Preparation

Preheat the oven to 180°C (350°F/Gas 4) and grease a 20 cm (8 in) square cake tin with butter or
sunflower oil.

Melt the butter and chocolate in a medium saucepan over a low heat, stirring gently. Remove
from the heat and stir in 165 g (5¾ oz/¾ cup) of the sugar and 1 teaspoon of the vanilla extract.
Beat in the whole eggs, one at a time, then stir in the flour and salt. Pour the batter into the
prepared tin and bake for 20 minutes.

While the brownies bake, mix together the egg white, remaining sugar, coconut and the other
teaspoon of vanilla extract.

When the brownies are ready, gently spread the coconut mixture over the top of them. Heat the
grill to its highest setting and grill the coconut-topped brownies, watching closely, until golden on
top. Cut into squares. These brownies can be served warm or at room temperature, on their own
or with vanilla or coconut ice cream.

STICKY BANOFFEE CAKE
with Salted Caramel

[SERVES 9–12]

So you know those two incredible desserts, sticky toffee pudding and banoffee pie?
Well, meet their delicious, hybrid baby. I made this cake for my friend who is obsessed with both
of those desserts. When I told her about the cake I couldn't move for about five minutes due to the
enthusiastic air-punching going on all around me. I think she was happy.
Note: If you're going all out, you can drizzle the cake with some melted dark
(bittersweet) chocolate too.

Ingredients

150 g (5 oz/1 cup) pitted dates, chopped
80 ml (3 fl oz/⅓ cup) vegetable oil
150 g (5 oz/¾ cup) light brown sugar
2 eggs
2 tbsp yoghurt
2 overripe bananas, peeled
1 tsp bicarbonate of soda (baking soda)
½ tsp salt
260 g (9¼ oz/2 cups) wholemeal
   (whole-wheat) flour

The Salted Caramel (as shown on page 187)

3½ tbsp granulated sugar
1 tbsp salted butter
4 tbsp whipping cream
flaky salt or fleur de sel, for sprinkling

Preparation

Soak the dates in 125 ml (4 fl oz/½ cup) boiling water for
10 minutes. Preheat the oven to 180°C (350°F/Gas 4) and liberally
grease a deep 20 cm (8 in) cake tin with butter or sunflower oil.

Place the dates and their soaking water in a food processor
and blitz until as smooth as possible. Add the oil, sugar, eggs,
yoghurt and bananas, blending until well combined. Blend in the
bicarbonate of soda, salt and flour until just mixed together.
Pour the batter into the prepared cake tin and bake for
40–50 minutes until well risen and a toothpick inserted into the
centre of the cake comes out clean. Leave to cool for
10 minutes before turning the cake onto a wire rack, with a

piece of baking parchment underneath the rack.

To make the caramel, heat the sugar with 4 tablespoons of
water in a deep saucepan, stirring until the sugar just dissolves.
Continue to heat the mixture, swirling the pan often, but not
stirring. Let it caramelise so that the mixture is mostly golden with
a few darker areas around the edges of the pan. Add the butter
and cream (be careful as it may spit and bubble up), turn down
the heat to low and stir until a smooth consistency is achieved.
Cook the caramel for a further 5 minutes to help it thicken, then
immediately pour it all over the cake. Sprinkle with the salt and
leave to cool and set.

· BROWNED BUTTER ·
Crumble Blue-barb Pie

[SERVES 8-10]

I am a rhubarb hoarder. There's always a surplus of it from the allotment and I make
sure that I chop some up to be frozen. If you treat it well, rhubarb is amazing for making pies. It naturally
contains quite a lot of liquid and has a pretty tart flavour, though, meaning you need something to absorb
the excess liquid (hopefully not the pastry underneath) and something to sweeten it. I mix
some of the crumble mixture into the filling for this purpose, and this has bonus points (!) because it also
makes the filling buttery and gooey. It's just perfect. As well as fresh blueberries I have added dried
blueberries to the mixture, which absorb some of the liquid as the pie bakes, plumping them back up.

Ingredients

½ quantity of Flaky Pastry (page 177)
  (allow the pastry to chill for at least
  30 minutes)
80 g (2¾ oz/6 tbsp) unsalted butter
90 g (3 oz/¾ cup) plain (all-purpose) flour
¼ tsp salt

1 tsp ground cinnamon
110 g (3¾ oz/½ cup) granulated sugar
30 g (1 oz/⅓ cup) walnuts, chopped
125 g (4½ oz/1 cup) blueberries
220 g (7¾ oz/2 cups) chopped rhubarb
50 g (2 oz/⅓ cup) dried blueberries (optional)

Preparation

Preheat the oven to 180°C (350°F/Gas 4). Roll out the chilled
pastry and use it to line a 20 cm (8 in) pie dish (as shown on pages
192–3). Prick the pastry all over with a fork. Crumple up a piece
of baking parchment about twice the size of your pie dish,
un-crumple it, and place it in the pastry-lined dish with a generous
handful of baking beans or rice. Blind bake the pastry for
10 minutes, then remove the baking parchment and baking beans
or rice and bake for a further 5 minutes. Remove from the oven
but leave the oven on.

Over a medium heat, melt the butter in a saucepan until it foams
and smells nutty. Remove the pan from the heat and stir in the flour,
salt, cinnamon and half the sugar. Mix the chopped walnuts into
this crumbly mixture.

In a large bowl, stir together the blueberries, rhubarb and
dried blueberries (if using) along with the remaining sugar and
3 tablespoons of the crumbly mixture. Pour into the pre-baked
pastry case and smooth into an even layer. Bake for 20 minutes,
then remove from the oven and cover with the rest of the crumbly
mixture. Return the pie to the oven for a further 20 minutes. Serve
with whipped cream or vanilla ice cream.

PEAR, FRANGIPANE &
Caramel Tartlets

[MAKES 12 TARTLETS]

Tartlets can often seem daunting and time consuming. I don't get much of a thrill from cutting out twenty-five pastry circles and fighting to get them into and out of their tartlet tins undamaged. Then decorating them all? Forget it. I'm tired just thinking about it. That's why these tartlets are so glorious: they're large enough so I don't feel the need to inhale five at a time, they take advantage of their ingredients' natural qualities for decoration and there are no tartlet pans involved, meaning they aren't super-fussy to make.

Ingredients

1 quantity of *Wholemeal Pastry* (page 178)
or 250 g (9 oz) store-bought shortcrust pastry
1 quantity of *Frangipane* (page 183)

6 small pears, halved and cored
3 tbsp granulated sugar
3 tbsp pistachios, finely chopped

Preparation

Preheat the oven to 180°C (350°F/Gas 4). On a lightly floured piece of baking parchment, roll out the pastry to a thickness of about 3 mm (⅛ in). Use a 9 cm (3½ in) pastry ring to cut out 12 pastry circles. Transfer the circles to a baking tray lined with baking parchment.

Top each pastry circle with a generous teaspoon of the frangipane and spread it out evenly. Finely slice the pear halves and use half a sliced pear to decorate each tartlet. Bake for 10 minutes until the pastry has darkened around the edges.

Heat the sugar with 2 tablespoons of water in a saucepan over a medium heat. Stir until the sugar has just dissolved, then stop stirring. Swirl the mixture, tilting the pan over a high heat until the sugar caramelises and the mixture is completely golden with some darker patches around the edges. Immediately remove the pan from the heat and use a pastry brush to dab the caramel over the baked tartlets. Sprinkle with the chopped pistachios and leave to cool.

CHAPTER SIX

STAPLES

+ How-To's

THESE ARE the basic recipes that I use all the time. They're simple, easy and totally customisable. If you've got a good base of solid recipes to rely on like these, you can create endless variations of them. Pastry and bread doughs are some of the most obvious, but things like nut butters, pesto and ganache are also very simple but powerful recipes that you can manipulate. They are (sometimes quite literally) the 'bread and butter' of recipes.

HERBY KALE Pesto

[MAKES 1 JAR/175 ML (6 FL OZ)]

This pesto is an essential pantry staple for me. It's incredibly easy to make and packs a nice, herby punch to any dish. If you don't have any kale around (or are not a fan) you can easily sub in rocket, spinach, watercress or extra basil. Same goes for the nuts — cashews, pistachios, hazelnuts, almonds or pine nuts (pine kernels) are just as good! As 'pesto' literally means 'paste', you can add in other goodies too, like wild garlic, roasted red peppers, sun-dried tomatoes, charred aubergines, asparagus and so on. I'll advise you now to make a huge batch and store the extra in the freezer — that way you're always pesto-ready, and that's the way to live right.

Ingredients

1 lemon
1 garlic clove, peeled and minced
100 g (3½ oz) kale, chopped
a large handful of basil leaves
4 tbsp olive oil

2 tbsp grated Parmesan
a large pinch of salt
30 g (1 oz) walnut halves

Preparation

Zest the lemon and cut it in half. Add the juice of one half to the bowl of a food processor with the zest. Add the minced garlic along with the remaining pesto ingredients. Blend until a paste forms. Use immediately or store in a lidded container in the fridge or freezer.

FLAKY PASTRY
Step-by-Step

[MAKES ENOUGH FOR 2 PIE CRUSTS]

This is the pastry to end all pastries. It's buttery in the best way possible and has the most desirably flaky texture I've ever achieved. The key is having different sized pieces of butter in the mixture when you add the liquids. That way some of the butter is being used to coat the flour granules so the pastry stays tender, and some is rolled into layers between the pastry which gives it a flaky texture. If you're making a pie, use this pastry and you will forget all about any previous shortcrust days.

Ingredients

320 g (11¼ oz/2½ cups) plain (all-purpose)
  flour
1 tsp salt
3 tbsp granulated sugar (if making sweet pastry)

200 g (7 oz/¾ cups plus 2 tbsp) unsalted butter,
  very cold
4 tbsp plain yoghurt, buttermilk or cream cheese,
  chilled

Preparation

To make in a food processor: pulse together the flour, salt and sugar (if using). Cube the butter and pulse it in briefly so that there are some small and large chunks of butter in the mixture. Add the yoghurt and some water (starting with 2 tablespoons) and pulse it in, until the mixture just starts to come together (add another tablespoon of water if needed). Tip the dough on to a work surface and use your hands to pull it together into a ball. Divide in half, flatten into discs and wrap in plastic wrap. Chill for at least 30 minutes (or for up to 3 days), until needed.

To make by hand: In a large bowl, stir together the flour, salt and sugar (if using). Cube the butter, add it to the bowl and rub it into the dry ingredients so that there are some smaller and larger chunks of butter in the mixture. Add the yoghurt and some water (starting with 2 tablespoons) and mix it in, until the dough starts to come together (add extra water if needed). Use your hands to press it together in the bowl. Divide in half, flatten into discs and wrap in plastic wrap. Chill for at least 30 minutes (or for up to 3 days), until needed.

The wrapped discs of pastry can also be frozen for up to a month.

WHOLEMEAL *Pastry*

[**MAKES 1 TART OR 10-12 TARTLETS**]

Using wholemeal (whole-wheat) flour in pastry gives it a nutty flavour while allowing you to feel virtuously wholesome when you eat it. It's easy to substitute all manner of other flours for the wholemeal, too. I like using spelt, buckwheat, einkorn or rye flour occasionally for a different flavour or texture. It's a good way to use up remnants of any rogue flours left over from recipe experiments. The coconut oil is a perfect fit for this pastry, giving it a short texture but keeping it suitable for vegans. If you're not a vegan you can of course use butter instead!

Ingredients

115 g (3⅔ oz/1 cup) wholemeal
    (whole wheat) flour
100 g (3½ oz/¾ cup, plus 1 tbsp)
    plain (all-purpose) flour

½ tsp salt
2 tbsp demerara (raw) sugar
    (if making sweet pastry)
100 g (3½ oz) coconut oil

Preparation

To make in a food processor: pulse together the flours, salt and sugar (if using). Pulse in the coconut oil until a crumbly texture is achieved. Add some cold water, starting with 2 tablespoons and pulse until the mixture starts to come together (add up to 2 tablespoons more water as needed). Tip the contents onto a work surface and use your hands to pull it together into a ball. Divide in half, flatten into discs and wrap in plastic wrap. Chill for at least 30 minutes (or for up to 3 days), until needed.

To make by hand: in a large bowl stir together the flours, salt and sugar (if using) with your hands. Add the coconut oil and rub it into the dry ingredients using your fingertips, until the mixture has a crumbly texture. Add some water, starting with 2 tablespoons and work it into the mixture until it starts to come together (add up to 2 tablespoons more water as needed). Use your hands to pull it together into a ball in the bowl. Divide in half, flatten into discs and wrap in plastic wrap. Chill for at least 30 minutes (or for up to 3 days), until needed.

The wrapped discs of pastry can also be frozen for up to a month.

· NO-KNEAD ·
Flatbread Dough

[**MAKES 1 MEDIUM LOAF, 2 PIZZAS OR 10-12 SMALL FLATBREADS**]

As much as I love kneading dough, there's a time and place for it. When it comes to long-rest flatbreads, it turns out that just stirring the dough together briefly is best. The high hydration and long resting period lets the gluten develop enough for flatbreads. It also means you get one bad-ass dough with a load of flavour (those yeast cells have been working hard!) and a chewy, open texture.

Ingredients

100 g (3½ oz/¾ cup) wholemeal (whole-wheat) bread flour

200 g (7 oz/1½ cups) plain (all-purpose) flour

¾ tsp salt

1 tsp active dried yeast

Preparation

In a large bowl, stir together the flours, salt and yeast. Add 225 ml (7¾ oz/1 cup minus 2 tbsp) lukewarm water and stir together with your hands until no floury patches remain. Cover with plastic wrap and leave in a warm place to rise for at least 2 hours. If you're leaving the dough for longer than 10 hours, put it in the fridge to rise slowly until needed.

BASIC BREAD
Dough

[**MAKES ENOUGH FOR 1 LARGE LOAF OR 12 ROLLS**]

'You have to LOVE the dough.' This is what my mum tells anyone any time they make simple bread dough. What she means by this is knead it by hand; leave the machines out of it. It will literally take ten minutes of your time and I promise you, will ensure a better loaf. It's 100 per cent mum-guaranteed (and no one can argue with their mum about this kind of thing).

Ingredients

450 g (1 lb/3½ cups) plain (all-purpose) flour, plus more for kneading (or use half plain and half wholemeal/whole-wheat flour)

7 g (½ oz) sachet dried yeast

1 tbsp honey or sugar (use 4 tbsp for a sweet recipe)

1½ tsp salt

1 egg

Preparation

In a large bowl, stir together the flour, yeast, honey or sugar and salt. Make a well in the centre of the ingredients, crack in the egg and pour in 250 ml (8½ fl oz/1 cup) lukewarm water. Stir with your hands, then tip out onto a lightly floured surface. Knead the dough for 10 minutes, adding a little more flour if needed, until you have a smooth, slightly sticky ball of dough.

Oil the bowl and place the dough in it. Cover with a clean kitchen towel and leave to rise in a warm place for 1 hour, or until doubled in size.

FRANGIPANE

[**MAKES ENOUGH FOR 1 CAKE
OR 12 TARTLETS**]

If you ever have fruit sitting around and are wondering what to do with it, think of frangipane. It will never let you down — it works especially well with stone fruits and berries. Fill tarts, spread onto brioche or swirl into cakes then top with some fruit and bake. It's no secret that I will eat frangipane batter from the bowl or that I've tainted cashew butter with almond extract and brown sugar so I can feign the frangipane flavour on my toast for breakfast.

Ingredients

3 tbsp butter or 4 tbsp Almond Butter
   (storebought or homemade, page 190)
50 g (2 oz/¼ cup) light brown sugar
1 tsp almond extract

1 egg
2 tbsp plain (all-purpose) flour
¼ tsp salt
45 g (1¾ oz/½ cup) ground almonds

Preparation

Cream together the butter (or almond butter), sugar, almond extract and egg. Stir in the flour, salt and ground almonds until smooth.

CHOCOLATE
Ganache

[**MAKES 250 G (9 OZ/1¼ CUPS)**]

The most versatile and easy chocolate thing you can make, ganache is the sun in the solar system of the baking universe. Use it as a shiny glaze, scoop it into truffles, whisk it into a fluffy frosting, slather it on for fudge frosting, or thin it out with some milk for a fudge sauce.
Note: Full-fat coconut milk can be substituted for the double (heavy) cream to make a dairy-free version. Coconut milk ganache normally sets faster so may require shorter chilling times than the cream version.

Ingredients

250 g (9 oz) dark (bittersweet) or chocolate (minimum 60% cocoa solids)

200 ml (7 fl oz) double (heavy) cream

Preparation

Roughly chop the chocolate into small chunks. Heat the cream in a small saucepan until just boiling then remove from the heat and add the chopped chocolate. Let the mixture sit for 5 minutes then stir together until completely combined.

— If using for a glaze, you can use the ganache immediately.
— If using for a fudge frosting, chill the ganache for at least 30 minutes in the fridge until it's slightly firmer.
— If using for a whipped chocolate frosting, chill the ganache for at least 1 hour in the fridge until firm, then use an electric whisk or a stand mixer fitted with the whisk attachment to whip the ganache until light in texture with a paler colour.

· CHOCOLATE ·
Hazelnut Butter

[**MAKES 400 G (14 OZ/1½ CUP)**]

Chocolate spread has the transcendent ability to snazz up bread from a
breakfast staple into a dessert of your dreams. It's like a bread party dress: everyone will be jealous,
especially if that chocolate spread is flecked with hazelnut and topped with raspberry jam.
I'm getting off topic here — main point being: make this chocolate-hazelnut butter and
your toast life will improve tenfold.

Ingredients

150 g (5 oz/1 cup) hazelnuts

145 g (5 oz/1 cup) almonds

3 tbsp vegetable oil

100 g (3½ oz/⅔ cup) dark (bittersweet)
  chocolate chips, or chopped chocolate
  (minimum 60% cocoa solids)

honey, maple syrup, agave syrup or icing sugar
  (confectioners' sugar), to taste

salt, to taste

Preparation

Preheat the oven to 180°C (350°F/Gas 4). Place the hazelnuts on
a baking tray with a rim and roast for 8–10 minutes until fragrant
and their skins are starting to peel off. Tip the hot hazelnuts
onto a clean kitchen towel and rub with the towel to remove the
bitter skins.

Immediately transfer the hazelnuts, almonds and oil to the bowl
of a food processor. Blend for 10–20 minutes, stopping to scrape
down the sides of the food processor as needed. The nuts will
become mealy, then start to clump together and eventually will
smooth out into a more liquid texture.

If you can feel that the nut mixture is hot, add the chocolate
immediately and blend until completely melted. If the nut mixture
isn't hot, melt the chocolate in a small, heatproof bowl placed
over a pan of simmering water (make sure the bottom of the bowl
doesn't actually touch the hot water). Add the melted chocolate
to the food processor and blend in.

Season with a sweetener of your choice and salt, to taste.
Store in a clean, sterilised jar (it will keep for up to 3 weeks in
the fridge).

SALTED

Caramel Sauce

[MAKES 80 ML (2¾/⅓ CUP)]

I used to be slightly scared of caramelising sugar – I never knew what colour it should be and the use of candy thermometers put me off. After some trial and error, I found that it's actually not very hard to do! Especially when there are step-by-step pictures for colour guidance. If you're making this to serve as a sauce, I recommend doubling the quantities of all the ingredients (including the water in the method) so you'll have enough for a few people!

Ingredients

3½ tbsp granulated sugar

1 tbsp salted butter

4 tbsp whipping cream

flaky salt or fleur de sel, for sprinkling

Preparation

To make the caramel, heat the sugar with 4 tablespoons of water in a deep saucepan, stirring until the sugar just dissolves. Continue to heat the mixture, swirling the pan often, but not stirring. Let it càramelise so that the mixture is mostly golden with a few darker areas around the edges of the pan. Add the butter and cream (be careful as it may spit and bubble up), turn down the heat to low and stir until a smooth consistency is achieved. Cook the caramel for a further 5 minutes to help it thicken, then immediately pour it all over the cake. Sprinkle with the salt and leave to cool and set.

Venn Colmar Lamb (via Italy)

Whole leg of lamb 2.5kg   tomatoes + puree
1 kg onions - shallots?
6 red peppers
4 tbsp oil
6 cloves garlic whole 1/2 head
1 bottle white wine + chile powder
Oregano ← polenta or pearl barley.
6 chillies (perhaps) deseeded & fried.
1. Brown seasoned meat in large pan/roasting tin.
2. Cut up peppers/onions & garlic, and sautée in large casserole 15 mins +
3. Add meat and wine to casserole & oregano +puree and cook @ 170° for 3 hrs covered in foil. Remove top and reduce for further hour if necessary.
4 Cut meat into chunks & serve with polenta.

A Dream OF A Gingerbread recipe

Gary Rhodes' Dreams COME ALIVE

"One of my favourite stories when I was younger was The Gingerbread Man – and now it's one of my favourite recipes! To find out what fun they are to make, just follow my recipe below and you'll end up with biscuits which taste delicious whatever shape you decide to make them into"

ALL YOU HAVE TO DO IS

Pre-heat oven to 180-200°C/350-400°F/gas mark 4-6 and grease two baking sheets.
Sift together flour, salt, soda and spices. Heat butter, sugar and syrup until dissolved. Leave to cool. Once cooled, mix into the dry ingredients with the evaporated milk to make a dough. Chill for 30 minutes.
Roll out the biscuit dough to about 5mm (1/4in) thick and cut into fingers, circles or even gingerbread men! Place on the baking sheets, allowing a little space to spread. Bake in pre-heated oven for 10-15 minutes.
MAKES ABOUT 20 BISCUITS.
"And, if you find yourself getting carried away in a gingerbread world of your own, why not take up the offer for my exclusive gingerbread baking kit. To see how, just see special packs for details."

ALL YOU NEED IS
100g (4 oz) Tate & Lyle dark brown soft cane sugar
100g (4 oz) Lyle's Golden Syrup
225g (8oz) plain flour
1/4 teaspoon salt
2 teaspoons bicarbonate of soda
1 heaped teaspoon ground ginger
1/2 teaspoon cinnamon
50g (2 oz) unsalted butter
1 tablespoon evaporated milk

Gary Rhodes

Smile It's Tate & Lyle

Chinese Plum Dip

1 pound purple plums or tinned
   fruit (pineapple, peaches, apricots)
2 Tbsp. soy sauce
2 Tbsp. vinegar
2 Tbsp. brown sugar
1/2 tsp. dry mustard
1/4 tsp. ground ginger
1/8 tsp. allspice
2 tsp. corn flour

Pit plums + put with syrup
and remaining ingredients
into blender. Puree and
pour into saucepan, cook
stirring until thickened.
Serve w/ chicken cutlets.

45

ALMOND
Butter

[MAKES 290 G (10½ OZ /1⅓ CUPS)]

The most basic of the nut butters made even more basic — the almonds are left untoasted.
I've found that some almond butters can taste bitter or are too strong to use subtly in baked goods
because the nuts are toasted first. I mean, dang, I just wanted to try to sneak some butter out of these
cookies and get some healthy fats in that dough, not make it taste like a peanut butter party. This
spread is plain and buttery so is perfect for adding creaminess (without the amount of dairy or saturated
fats that are present in dairy) to everything from soups to muffin batters.
Note: If you want, you can add maple syrup, sugar, honey or agave syrup and salt to taste,
once the nut butter is made.

Ingredients

290 g (10½ oz/1⅓ cups) almonds

Preparation

Place the almonds in the bowl of a food processor. Blend for 10–20 minutes, stopping to scrape
down the sides of the food processor as needed. The nuts will become mealy, then start to clump
together and eventually will smooth out into a more liquid texture. Store in a clean, sterilised jar
(it will keep for up to a month in the fridge).

SALTED

Treacle Butter

[**MAKES 110 G (3³/₄ OZ /¹/₂ CUP)**]

There is a kind of magic that happens when treacle and butter are combined with
a sprinkle of salt. All the flavours of a salty, muscovado caramel come together within seconds into
a bread-spreadable form. Try it on some toasted brioche with jam, spread on pancakes, or fry some
toasty croûtons in it to add an unexpected highlight of sweetness to autumnal salads.

Ingredients

110 g (3¾ oz/½ cup) unsalted butter, softened   ½ tsp flaky salt

2 tsp black treacle or unsulfured molasses

Preparation

Cream the butter together with the treacle until it has an even gold colour and a light texture.
Stir in the flaky salt and chill until needed.

. HOW TO .
Line a Pie Dish with Pastry

[**PREP TIME 10 MINS**]

Lightly flour a large piece of baking parchment. Place the pastry on it and flour that too.

Use a rolling pin to gently roll out the pastry, starting from the centre of the pastry and pushing out towards the edge. Rotate the parchment so you can turn the pastry easily and work your way around it, rolling in all directions so you end up with a circle (well, a circle as far as possible).

Keep rolling until it is larger than your pie dish.

Lightly flour the pastry and rolling pin, then roll the pastry up onto the rolling pin.

Unroll the pastry onto the pie dish.

Use your fingers to gently lift and push the pastry into the dish. You can use a little ball of excess pastry to help you push it in if you need to.

Fold up the edge and pinch to make a rim. I like to leave a bit of an overhang of pastry, as it will shrink slightly as it bakes.

For a decorative crust, pinch the dough between your thumb and bent forefinger at a 45-degree angle, all the way around the rim.

Once lined, it's best to chill the pastry for 30 minutes before blind baking so that the gluten can relax. This will prevent the crust from shrinking too much when it bakes.

. HOW TO .

Line, Grease and Flour Cake Tins

[PREP TIME 10 MINS]

Cut a square of baking parchment a little bigger than the size of your cake tin.

Fold the parchment square in half to form a rectangle.

Fold it in half again to form a small square.

Then fold in half one last time to form a triangle.

Place the triangle on the base of the upturned cake tin. Position it so that the thinnest, longest point is in the centre of the tin.

Trim it using the edge of the tin as a guide.

Unfold the baking parchment. It should fit the cake tin perfectly.

Grease the edge and base of the cake tin using a folded piece of kitchen paper and some softened butter, coconut oil, margarine or shortening. Alternatively, using a pastry brush or spray, grease with vegetable oil.

Smooth the circle of baking parchment into the cake tin.

Grease the baking parchment circle as you did the cake tin.

Sprinkle in a small amount of flour.

Tilt, turn and tap the tin to coat the edge and base with flour.

Tap on a work surface and pour out any excess flour into the bin.

. THANK YOU .

Kate Pollard, Kajal Mistry and the team at Hardie Grant — thank you
so much for believing in me right from the start and making this book
possible — you're the best! It has been a dream come true, and I'm so
happy that it was you guys that made this all happen.

Charlotte Heal — this book wouldn't even be half as special without your
amazing eye for design. You made it look even more perfect than I could
have ever imagined!

Mum and Dad — you've provided the encouragement, inspiration and all
the help and love I could ever need. Thank you for your amazing taste in
a) food b) design, and c) kitchenware which you've surrounded me with
for my whole life. You're so cool and I love you both too much for words.

Jasper — yeah, I used to yell at you when you wouldn't let me watch my
TV programmes but you are one of the best, most creative and awesome
people I know. Thanks for all the washing up, chopping and cycling to
the supermarket you did for me. I would've had a mental breakdown if
I didn't have your help, bro.

Sarah and the Apseys — my best friend and second family for practically
my whole life. I am so lucky to have your support and love.

Bea and Rhiannon — my clique! You've ruined my sense of humour with
too many inside jokes, awkward selfies and puns to count and I love you
so much for that. I'm glad that you were so easily bribed with cookies to
come and take photos of me.

Beattie, Elspeth, Phoebe, Annie, Sophie, Elsa — you played an extremely
important part in the creation of this book — thanks for taking care of the
excess cakes that I brought into school. I would've been buried alive in
baked goods otherwise. Your friendship means so much to me, even more
than bittersweet chocolate or Maldon salt, and that's something!

The readers of *Top With Cinnamon* — well, it was all of your incredible
support that helped me to get here! Thank you for reading, subscribing
and commenting on my blog. Without it, I may not have continued down
the path which has led me here today. You're amazing and I want to hug
you all.

ABOUT IZY

Izy Hossack is the student, recipe developer, food photographer and stylist behind the blog *Top With Cinnamon*, which she started in 2011. She is a self-taught cook who believes that maple syrup, flaky salt and dark chocolate are the answer to everything. Her work has been featured in many publications and websites such as *Cherry Bombe, Marie Claire, Frankie, Glamour, Elle, Buzzfeed, The Week, Food52* and *The Kitchn*. Her blog has been a finalist in *Saveur's* Best Food Blog awards in 2013 and 2014. In her spare time Izy enjoys cycling around London, eating far too much muesli and drinking cinnamon-sprinkled coffee out of mason jars.

Index

Index

Index

Index

Top With Cinnamon by Izy Hossack

First published in 2014 by Hardie Grant Books

Hardie Grant Books (UK)
Dudley House, North Suite
34–35 Southampton Street
London WC2E 7HF
www.hardiegrant.co.uk

Hardie Grant Books (Australia)
Ground Floor, Building 1
658 Church Street
Melbourne, VIC 3121
www.hardiegrant.com.au

British Library Cataloguing-in-Publication Data. A catalogue record
for this book is available from the British Library.

ISBN 978-174270-770-9

Publisher: Kate Pollard
Desk Editor: Kajal Mistry
Editor & proofreader: Laura Herring & Diana Vowls
Indexer: Cathy Davies
Cover and Internal Design: Charlotte Heal Design
Design Assistant: Kat Jenkins
Photography © Izy Hossack
Styling: Izy Hossack
Colour Reproduction by p2d

Find this book on Cooked.
Cooked.com.au
Cooked.co.uk

Printed and bound in China by 1010
10 9 8 7 6 5 4 3 2 1